Prepared in cooperation with the City of Brunswick and Glynn County

Groundwater Conditions and Studies in the Brunswick–Glynn County Area, Georgia, 2008

Open-File Report 2009–1275

U.S. Department of the Interior
U.S. Geological Survey

Groundwater Conditions and Studies in the Brunswick–Glynn County Area, Georgia, 2008

By Gregory S. Cherry, Michael F. Peck, Jaime A. Painter, and Welby L. Stayton

Prepared in cooperation with the City of Brunswick and Glynn County

Open-File Report 2009–1275

U.S. Department of the Interior
U.S. Geological Survey

U.S. Department of the Interior
KEN SALAZAR, Secretary

U.S. Geological Survey
Marcia K. McNutt, Director

U.S. Geological Survey, Reston, Virginia: 2010

For more information on the USGS—the Federal source for science about the Earth, its natural and living resources, natural hazards, and the environment, visit *http://www.usgs.gov* or call 1-888-ASK-USGS.

For an overview of USGS information products, including maps, imagery, and publications, visit *http://www.usgs.gov/pubprod*.

To order this and other USGS information products, visit *http://store.usgs.gov*.

Suggested citation:
Cherry, G.S., Peck, M.F., Painter, J.A., and Stayton, W.L., 2010, Groundwater conditions and studies in the Brunswick–Glynn County area, Georgia, 2008: U.S. Geological Survey Open-File Report 2009–1275, 54 p.

Contents

Figures

Tables

Conversion Factors and Datums

Multiply	By	To obtain
Length		
inch	2.54	centimeter (cm)
foot (ft)	0.3048	meter (m)
mile (mi)	1.609	kilometer (km)
Area		
square foot (ft^2)	0.09290	square meter (m^2)
square mile (mi^2)	2.590	square kilometer (km^2)
Volume		
gallon (gal)	3.785	liter (L)
Million gallons (Mgal)	3,785	cubic meter (m^3)

Temperature in degrees Celsius (°C) may be converted to degrees Fahrenheit (°F) as follows:

$$°F = (1.8 \times °C) + 32$$

Temperature in degrees Fahrenheit (°F) may be converted to degrees Celsius (°C) as follows:

$$°C = (°F - 32) / 1.8$$

Vertical coordinate information is referenced to the North American Vertical Datum of 1988 (NAVD 88).

Historical data collected and stored as National Geodetic Vertical Datum of 1929 (NGVD 29).

Horizontal coordinate information is referenced to the North American Datum of 1983 (NAD 83).

Altitude, as used in this report, refers to distance above the vertical datum.

Specific conductance is given in microsiemens per centimeter at 25 degrees Celsius (µS/cm at 25 °C).

Concentrations of chemical constituents in water are given either in milligrams per liter (mg/L) or micrograms per liter (µg/L).

Groundwater Conditions and Studies in the Brunswick–Glynn County Area, Georgia, 2008

By Gregory S. Cherry, Michael F. Peck, Jaime A. Painter, and Welby L. Stayton

Abstract

The Upper Floridan aquifer is contaminated with saltwater in a 2-square-mile area of downtown Brunswick, Georgia. This contamination has limited development of the groundwater supply in the Glynn County area. Hydrologic, geologic, and water-quality data are needed to effectively manage water resources. Since 1959, the U.S. Geological Survey has conducted a cooperative water program with the City of Brunswick to monitor and assess the effect of ground-water development on saltwater contamination of the Floridan aquifer system.

During calendar year 2008, the cooperative water program included continuous water-level recording of 12 wells completed in the Floridan, Brunswick, and surficial aquifer systems; collecting water levels from 21 wells to map the potentiometric surface of the Upper Floridan aquifer during July 2008; and collecting and analyzing water samples from 26 wells to map chloride concentrations in the Upper Floridan aquifer during July 2008. Equipment was installed on 3 wells for real-time water level and specific conductance monitoring. In addition, work was continued to refine an existing groundwater-flow model for evaluation of water-management scenarios.

Introduction

In the Brunswick, Georgia, area (fig. 1), saltwater has been contaminating the Upper Floridan aquifer for about 50 years. As of 2008, within a 2-square-mile (mi^2) area in downtown Brunswick, the aquifer yielded water with a chloride concentration greater than 2,000 milligrams per liter (mg/L), which exceeds the State and Federal secondary drinking-water standard of 250 mg/L (Georgia Environmental Protection Division, 1997; U.S. Environmental Protection Agency, 2000). Saltwater contamination has limited further development of the Upper Floridan aquifer in the Brunswick area, prompting interest in the development of alternative sources of water supply, primarily from the shallower surficial and Brunswick aquifer systems. Monitoring groundwater conditions and conducting studies to better define the occurrence of saltwater contamination and assess alternative water sources is important for management of the water resources in the Brunswick–Glynn County area.

Brunswick–Glynn County Cooperative Water Program

The Cooperative Water Program (CWP) between the U.S. Geological Survey (USGS) and the City of Brunswick and Glynn County has been in existence since 1959. Current cooperating entities are the Joint Water and Sewer Commission (JWSC) and the Jekyll Island Authority. The CWP was initiated in response to concerns about chloride contamination of the Upper Floridan aquifer, which first became evident during the late 1950s. Since its inception, the CWP has placed emphasis on providing the necessary information about the Floridan aquifer system to manage saltwater intrusion and evaluate water-resources data.

Purpose and Scope

Hydrologic, geologic, and water-quality data are needed to effectively manage water resources in the coastal area of Georgia. During calendar year 2008, the CWP, which includes all of Glynn County (fig. 1), continued and included continuous water-level monitoring of 12 wells completed in the Floridan, Brunswick, and surficial aquifer systems. Water levels also were collected from 21 wells to map the potentiometric surface of the Upper Floridan aquifer during July 2008. In addition, water samples were collected and analyzed from 26 wells in order to assess the configuration of the chloride plume in the Upper Floridan aquifer near the City of Brunswick during July 2008. Work was continued to refine an existing groundwater-flow model (Payne and others, 2005) in order to evaluate selected water-management scenarios.

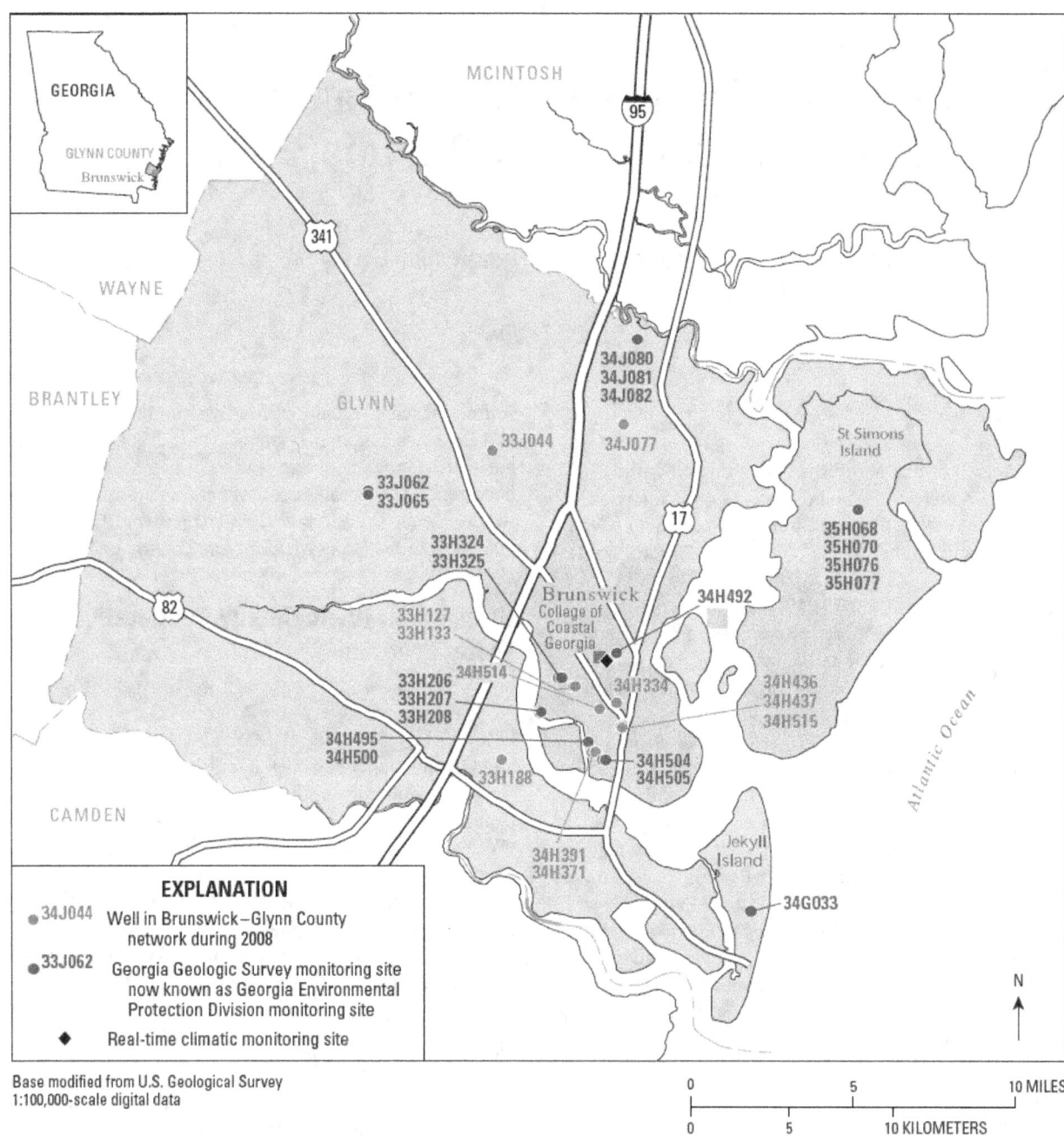

Figure 1.   Location of study area and continuous groundwater-level monitoring network for the Brunswick–Glynn County area, Georgia.

Acknowledgments

The authors appreciate the technical feedback and guidance provided by the Brunswick–Glynn County Water Resources Management Advisory Committee (WRMAC). Several USGS employees played an important role in the collection, processing, and quality assurance of groundwater data, including Alan M. Cressler, Michael Hamrick, Jamal A. Grimes, and Christopher B. Walls. Appreciation is extended to Dorothy F. Payne for consultation and advice during development of a groundwater-flow model for the Brunswick–Glynn County area and assistance with water-quality sampling. Cartography and layout were by Caryl J. Wipperfurth and Bonnie J. Turcott.

Groundwater Conditions

Groundwater levels and chloride concentrations in the Brunswick–Glynn County area have been monitored for several decades as part of the CWP. Precipitation and ground-water pumpage are monitored to assess their influence on groundwater conditions. These data can be used to guide water-management decisions by State and local authorities.

Groundwater Levels

During calendar year 2008, groundwater levels in the Brunswick–Glynn County area were continuously monitored by the USGS in 32 wells—12 wells were funded through the CWP and 20 wells were funded through a similar program with the Georgia Department of Natural Resources, Environmental Protection Division (GaEPD) (fig. 1; table 1). Of the 32 continuous water-level recorders, 12 are completed in the Upper Floridan aquifer, 8 in the Lower Floridan aquifer, 7 in the Brunswick aquifer system, and 5 in the surficial aquifer system (table 1).

Real-time water-level monitoring systems were installed in wells completed in the upper and (or) lower water-bearing zones of the Upper Floridan aquifer that surround the area of chloride contamination—Southside Baptist Church (34H504 and 34H505), Perry Park (34H514), and Georgia–Pacific Cellulose (33H324 and 33H325). These sites were then adapted for real-time specific conductance monitoring in the upper and lower water-bearing zones of the Upper Floridan aquifer.

Factors Influencing Groundwater Levels

Fluctuations and long-term trends in groundwater levels occur as a result of changes in recharge to and discharge from an aquifer. Recharge rates vary in response to precipitation, evapotranspiration, and surface-water infiltration into an aquifer. Discharge occurs as natural flow from an aquifer to streams or springs, as evapotranspiration from shallow water-table aquifers, as leakage to vertically adjacent aquifers, and as withdrawal (pumpage) from wells. When recharge to an aquifer exceeds discharge, groundwater levels rise; when discharge from an aquifer exceeds recharge, groundwater levels decline. Water levels generally are highest in the winter to early spring when precipitation is greatest, evapotranspiration is lowest, and irrigation withdrawals are minimal; water levels are the lowest during summer and fall when evapotranspiration and pumpage are greatest (Payne and others, 2005).

Hydrographs from the monitoring network are presented here to compare 2008 trends and seasonal fluctuations to period-of-record statistics in major aquifers of coastal Georgia. Additional well information can be obtained from the USGS National Water Information System (NWIS) at *http://waterdata.usgs.gov/ga/nwis/gw/*.

Maps of the monitoring network are presented showing the areal distribution of observation wells for each of the major aquifers of coastal Georgia and a comparison of 2008 median water levels to period of record normal water levels. This analysis is similar to that performed for a USGS report on groundwater conditions in Georgia in which the period-of-record comparisons must be greater than 3 years (Peck and others, 2009). For this analysis, the normal range is defined as water-level observations during the calendar year that were between the 25th and 75th percentiles for the period of record. The 75th percentile means that three-quarters of the observations lie below it; the 25th percentile means that one-quarter of the observations lie below it; and the median or 50th percentile means that one-half of the observations lie below and one-half lie above. These comparisons were used to determine if water levels were above normal, below normal, or normal, and water levels then are shown graphically on the maps. An arrow pointing upward for 2008 represents monthly mean water levels above period-of-record normal values, an arrow pointing downward for 2008 represents monthly mean water levels below period-of-record normal values, and a circle for 2008 represents monthly mean water levels within the period-of-record normal values.

Precipitation

Precipitation in the Brunswick–Glynn County area influences groundwater levels in the shallow surficial aquifer system and, to a lesser degree, in the Brunswick aquifer system. In addition, changes in precipitation affect quantities of groundwater that can be withdrawn from deeper aquifers and, therefore, have an indirect effect on groundwater levels in the Upper Floridan aquifer. Rainfall is not evenly distributed throughout the year, and maximum rainfall generally occurs during the summer months of June, July, and August (Payne and others, 2005) when tropical systems associated with the hurricane season may produce heavy rainfall along the coast. A real-time climatic monitoring site was established as part of the CSSI on the College of Coastal Georgia campus at Brunswick to monitor precipitation in the Brunswick–Glynn County area (fig. 1). Real-time monitoring data for this site are accessible on the Web at *www.georgiaweather.net* (accessed on May 29, 2009).

Precipitation data and cumulative departure from normal during 2000–2008 are shown in figure 2. The cumulative departure from normal precipitation for the period of record can be used to evaluate trends in precipitation, which typically relate to recharge of shallow aquifers. Cumulative departure depicts the long-term surplus or deficit of precipitation during a designated period and is derived by adding successive values of departure from normal precipitation. In this report, normal precipitation for a given day is defined as the average of total daily precipitation during the period of record (2000–2008). A downward trend in the cumulative departure line indicates a period of below-normal precipitation, whereas an upward trend indicates above-normal precipitation.

Table 1. Brunswick–Glynn County, Georgia, groundwater-level monitoring network, 2008.

Site name	Aquifer	Subunit	Year began
34H515*	Surficial	Deeper (confined) zone	2005
34H437	Upper Brunswick	None	1983
34J077	Upper Brunswick	None	1998
33H127	Upper Floridan	Lower water-bearing zone	1962
33H133	Upper Floridan	Upper water-bearing zone	1964
34H334	Upper Floridan	Lower water-bearing zone	1962
34H371	Upper Floridan	Upper water-bearing zone	1967
34H514**	Upper Floridan	Upper water-bearing zone	2007
33H188	Lower Floridan	Fernandina permeable zone	1978
33J044	Lower Floridan	Undifferentiated	1979
34H391	Lower Floridan	Brackish water zone	1970
34H436	Lower Floridan	Brackish water zone	1983
Additional wells (funded by Georgia Environmental Protection Division)			
33H208	Surficial	Deeper (confined) zone	1983
34H492	Surficial	Water-table zone	1999
34J082	Surficial	None	2002
35H076	Surficial	Deeper (confined) zone	2007
33J065	Upper Brunswick	None	2001
34J081	Upper Brunswick	None	2002
33J062	Lower Brunswick	None	2001
34J080	Lower Brunswick	None	2002
35H077	Lower Brunswick	None	2005
33H207	Upper Floridan	Upper water-bearing zone	1983
33H324**	Upper Floridan	Upper water-bearing zone	2007
33H325**	Upper Floridan	Lower water-bearing zone	2007
34G033	Upper Floridan	None	2004
34H504**	Upper Floridan	Upper water-bearing zone	2007
34H505**	Upper Floridan	Lower water-bearing zone	2007
35H070	Upper Floridan	Upper water-bearing zone	2007
33H206	Lower Floridan	Brackish water zone	1983
34H495	Lower Floridan	Fernandina permeable zone	2001
34H500	Lower Floridan	Fresh water-bearing zone	2001
35H068	Lower Floridan	Fresh water-bearing zone	2007

*Replaces 34H438

** Real-time station

Cumulative departure data from the Coastal Georgia Community College in Brunswick, indicate a period of below-normal precipitation from January 2000 to May 2002, corresponding to a drought period that began during the middle of 1998 (Barber and Stamey, 2000). Between June 2004 and October 2005, precipitation was mostly above normal with one short period of below-normal precipitation between October 2004 and February 2005.

Rainfall was mostly below normal from October 2005 through December 2008 (fig. 2A). The maximum amount of rainfall recorded in a 24-hour period was 6.05 inches on October 5, 2005 (fig. 2B). During a 6-day period (October 2–7, 2005), rainfall, associated with Tropical Storm Tammy, totaled nearly 18 inches in the area, and the cumulative departure increased from 10 inches to more than 27 inches (fig. 2A).

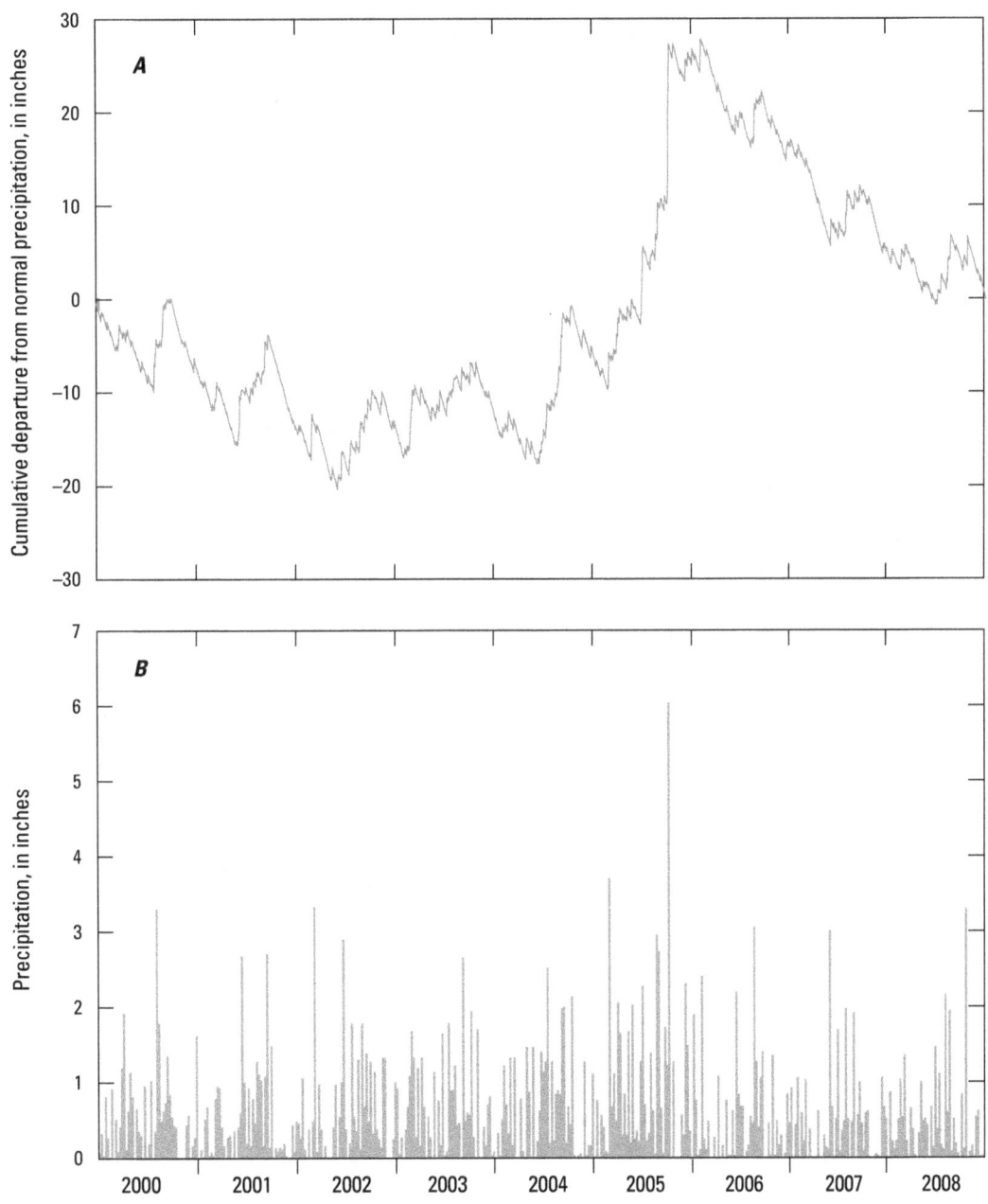

Figure 2.   *(A)* Cumulative departure from normal precipitation and *(B)* total daily precipitation at real-time climatic monitoring site, College of Coastal Georgia Georgia January 2000–December 2008 (see figure 1 for location).

Groundwater Pumpage

The locations of groundwater pumping centers and amounts of water withdrawn from these centers may substantially affect groundwater levels in the Brunswick–Glynn County area. Changes in pumping rates and the addition of new pumping centers may alter the configuration of potentiometric surfaces, reverse groundwater-flow directions, and increase seasonal and long-term fluctuations in the aquifers. During 2008, about 47 million gallons per day (Mgal/d) was withdrawn from the Upper Floridan aquifer in Glynn County, of which 8.76 Mgal/d was for public supply and 38.1 Mgal/d was for industry (Julia Fanning, U.S. Geological Survey, written commun., May 2009). According to Payne and others (2005), pumpage from the Upper Floridan aquifer in Glynn County decreased from 95.4 Mgal/d during 1980 to 61.1 Mgal/d during 2000, reflecting increased water conservation by local industry.

Historically, groundwater pumpage peaked in the early 1980s with the majority of groundwater withdrawals used for industrial purposes (fig. 3). In calendar year 1980, Georgia–Pacific Cellulose and Ashland Aqualon (formerly Hercules–Pinova) withdrew a total of 78.3 Mgal/d; groundwater withdrawals for public supply averaged 9.8 Mgal/d (L.E. Jones, U.S. Geological Survey, written commun., March 2007). At Ashland Aqualon, groundwater pumpage reached a maximum of 24 Mgal/d during 1970, and in 1982 pumpage was reduced to 14 Mgal/d due to water-conservation measures at the facility and the construction of a cooling tower (L.E. Jones, U.S. Geological Survey, written commun., March 2007). Georgia–Pacific Cellulose implemented similar water-conservation measures in the early 1990s and reduced groundwater pumpage from 58.8 Mgal/d during 1980 to 33.1 Mgal/d

during 2005 (L.E. Jones, U.S. Geological Survey written commun., March, 2007). During 2001–2008, pumpage from the Upper Floridan aquifer at the Georgia–Pacific Cellulose plant decreased by nearly 5 Mgal/d, while pumpage at the Ashland Aqualon plant decreased by nearly 2 Mgal/d. Public supply for the City of Brunswick, Sea Island, St. Simons Island, and Jekyll Island remained at about 9 Mgal/d during the same period (Julia Fanning, U.S. Geological Survey, written commun., May 2009; fig. 3). During 1980–2005, water use by local industries (Georgia–Pacific Cellulose and Ashland Aqualon) decreased by nearly half, from 78.3 Mgal/d during 1980 to 41.1 Mgal/d during 2005 (Fanning and Trent, 2009). The reduction in pumpage had a pronounced effect on groundwater levels in the area. During 2008, pumpage estimates indicated further reductions in groundwater withdrawals from the Upper Floridan aquifer at the Georgia–Pacific Cellulose plant of 1.2 Mgal/d and decreased pumpage at the Ashland Aqualon plant by about 2.3 Mgal/d for a combined total of 37.5 Mgal/d (Julia Fanning, U.S. Geological Survey, written commun., May 2009; fig. 3).

Water use for public supply steadily increased from 1940 to 1990 and leveled off through 2008 due to the rise in population within Glynn County, which has increased from 21,920 during 1940 to 75,884 during 2008 (U.S. Census Bureau, accessed May 29, 2009, at *http://www.census.gov/ popest/counties/CO-EST2008-01.html*). As a result, groundwater pumpage for public supply doubled from 4.4 Mgal/d during 1940 to 8.8 Mgal/d during 2008 (fig. 3). Despite the population increase, pumpage during 2008 is similar to pumpage during 1980 because of greater accountability in the water distribution systems, water conservation measures, and decreased losses due to system leakage (Keith Morgan, Brunswick–Glynn County Joint Water and Sewer Commission, oral commun., June 2009).

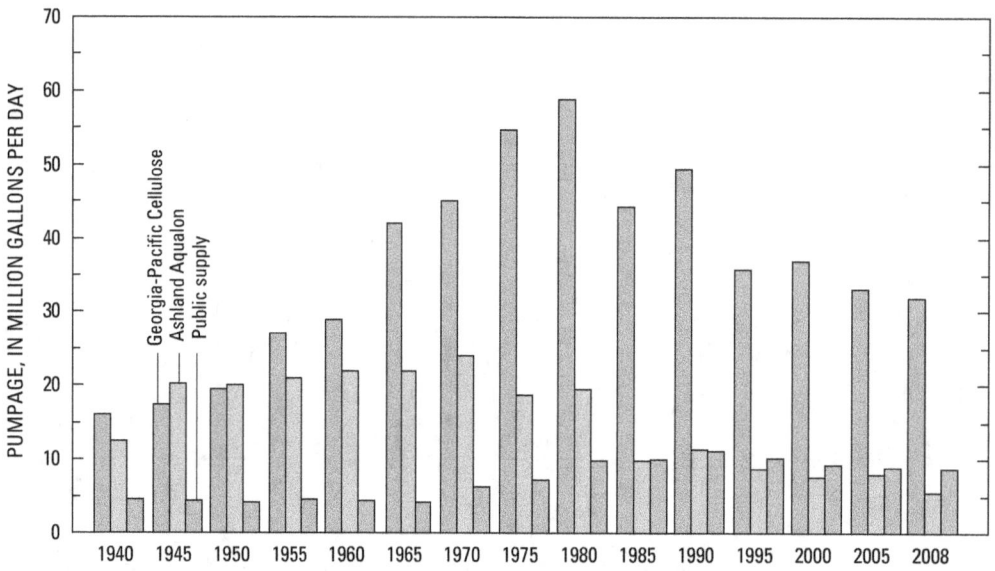

Figure 3. Major groundwater pumpage from the Upper Floridan aquifer in the Brunswick–Glynn County area, Georgia, 1940–2008.

Surficial Aquifer System

During 2008, water levels were monitored in five wells completed in the surficial aquifer system in the Brunswick–Glynn County area (fig. 4; table 1). Hydrographs for these wells are shown in figures 5–8 with the exception of well 35H076, which has insufficient record due to recent installation in early 2007. Mean water levels were mostly greater than the historical daily median in well 33H208 (fig. 5). Water levels were at or below historical daily median values for nearly all of 2008 in two of the four wells

(wells 34H492 and 34J082, figs. 6–7), corresponding to a period of largely below-normal precipitation from late 2005 through December 2008 (fig. 2). The period of record was too short in wells 34H515 (fig. 8) and 35H076 (fig. 4) for statistical comparisons to percentile ranges. The reason for the different water-level pattern at well 33H208 is unknown; however, it could be related to decreased pumpage at Georgia–Pacific Cellulose since 1990 (fig. 3) as the lowest water levels correspond to a period of greater pumpage during the late 1980s, or it could be caused by local variations in precipitation in the area.

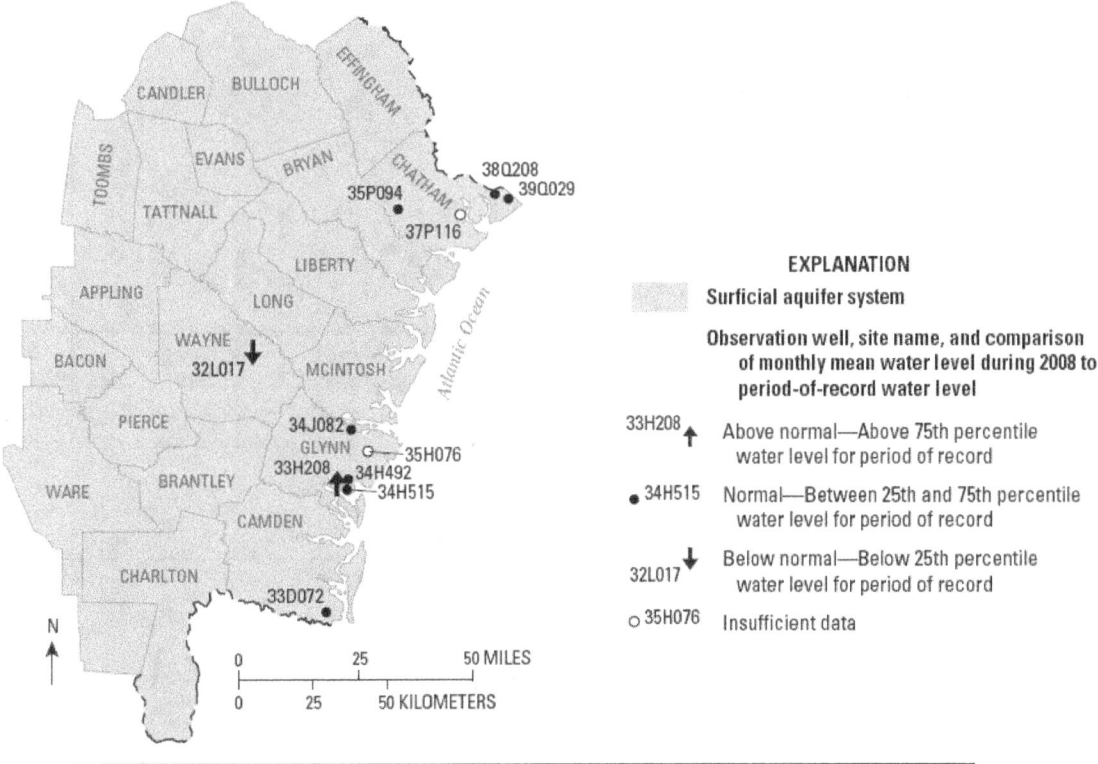

Site name	County	Other identifier[1]
33D072	Camden	Georgia Geologic Survey, St Marys, test well 3
35P094	Chatham	University of Georgia, Bamboo Farm well
37P116	Chatham	Georgia Geologic Survey, Skidaway Institute, test well 4
38Q208	Chatham	Fort Pulaski, Savannah Harbor Expansion, monitoring well 4, COE
39Q029	Chatham	Tybee, Savannah Harbor Expansion, monitoring well 1, COE
33H208	Glynn	Georgia–Pacific Cellulose, south test well 3
34H492	Glynn	Coastal Georgia Community College P-17
34H515	Glynn	Coffin Park test well 4
34J082	Glynn	Coastal Sound Science Initiative, Ebenezer Bend, AR-4
35H076	Glynn	Georgia Geologic Survey, St Simons
32L017	Wayne	Georgia Geologic Survey, Gardi, test well 3

[1] Georgia Geologic Survey now known as Georgia Environmental Protection Division
COE, U.S. Army Corps of Engineers

Figure 4.   Groundwater levels in the surficial aquifer system in the central and southern coastal areas, Georgia, 2008.

Surficial aquifer system

310925081312203   Site Name: **33H208**
Glynn County   Period of Record: 1983–2008
Well Depth: 155 feet   Datum: 7.00 feet NGVD 29   Well Diameter: 4.00 inches

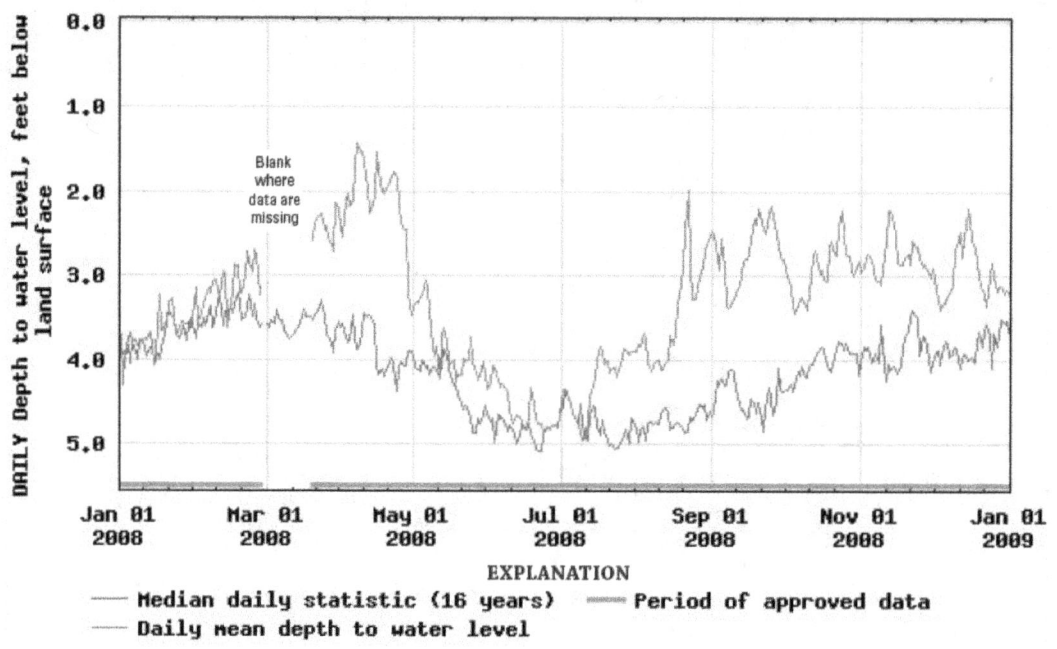

EXPLANATION
—— Median daily statistic (16 years)   ▬▬ Period of approved data
—— Daily mean depth to water level

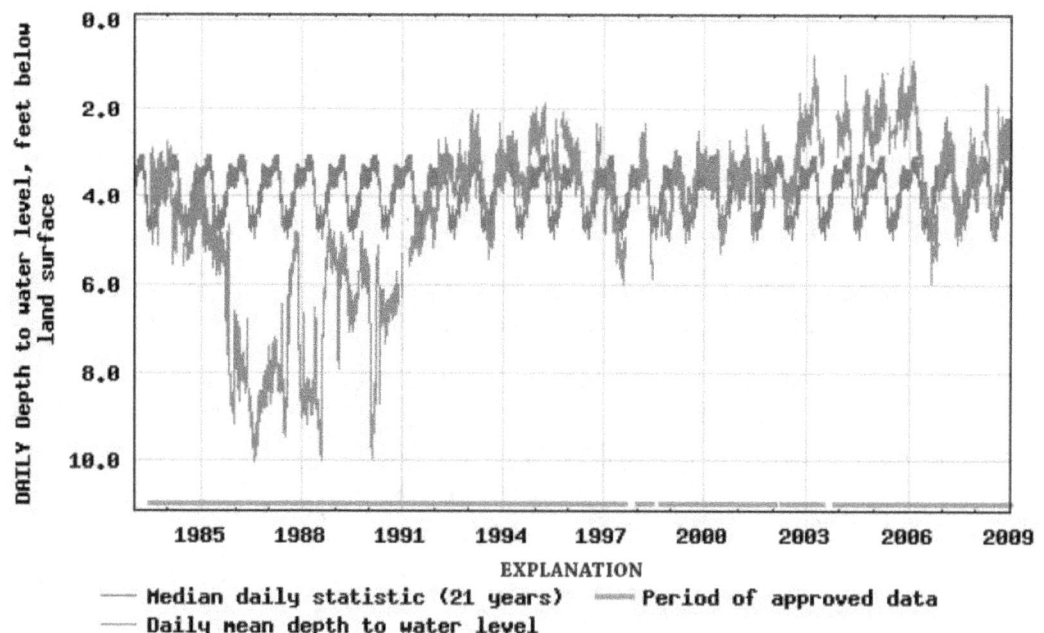

EXPLANATION
—— Median daily statistic (21 years)   ▬▬ Period of approved data
—— Daily mean depth to water level

Figure 5. Periodic and daily mean water levels in well 33H208, surficial aquifer system, Glynn County, Georgia, 1983–2008

Surficial aquifer system

311059081285702   Site Name: **34H492**
Glynn County   Period of Record: 1999–2008
Well Depth: 48.5 feet   Datum: 12.54 feet NGVD 29 Well Diameter: 2.00 inches

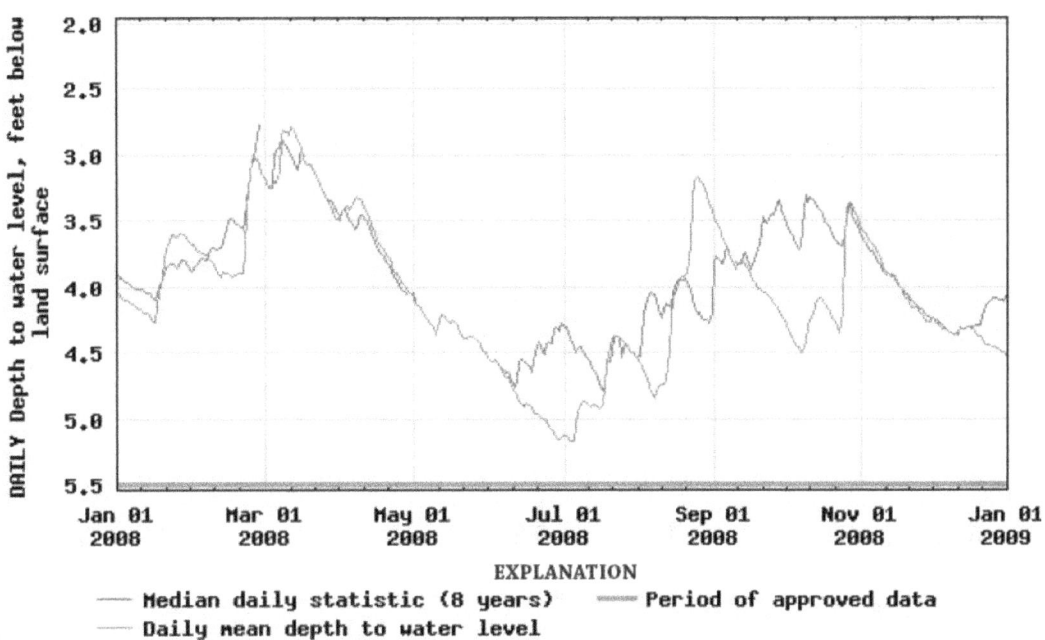

EXPLANATION
— Median daily statistic (8 years)   ▬▬ Period of approved data
— Daily mean depth to water level

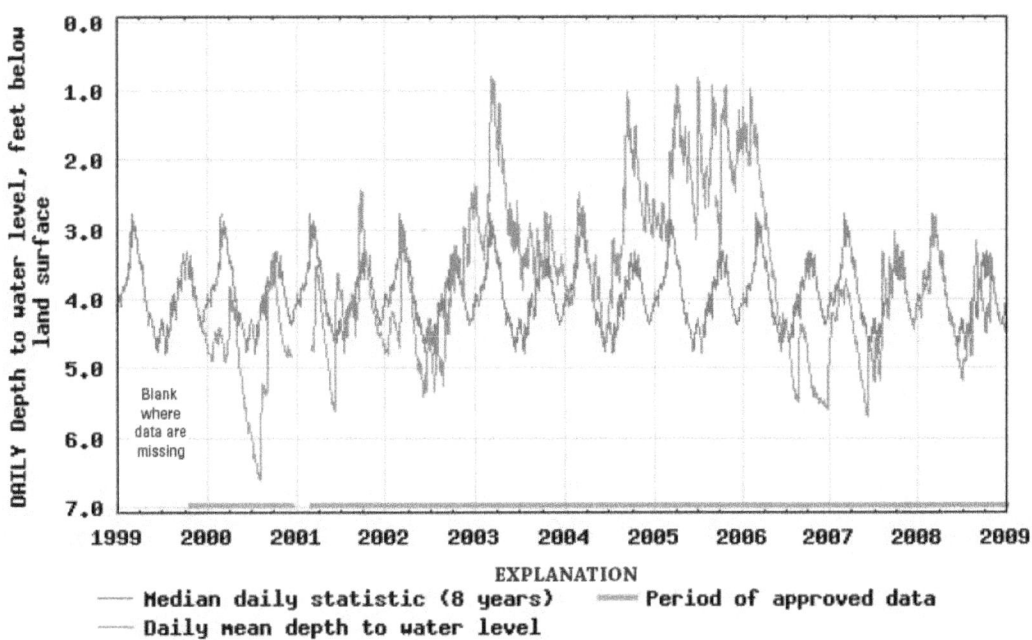

EXPLANATION
— Median daily statistic (8 years)   ▬▬ Period of approved data
— Daily mean depth to water level

Figure 6.   Periodic and daily mean water levels in well 34H492, surficial aquifer system, Glynn County, Georgia, 1999–2008.

Surficial aquifer system

311909081281103   Site Name: 34J082
Glynn County   Period of Record: 2002–2008
Well Depth: 160 feet   Datum: 15.90 feet NGVD 29   Well Diameter: 4.00 inches

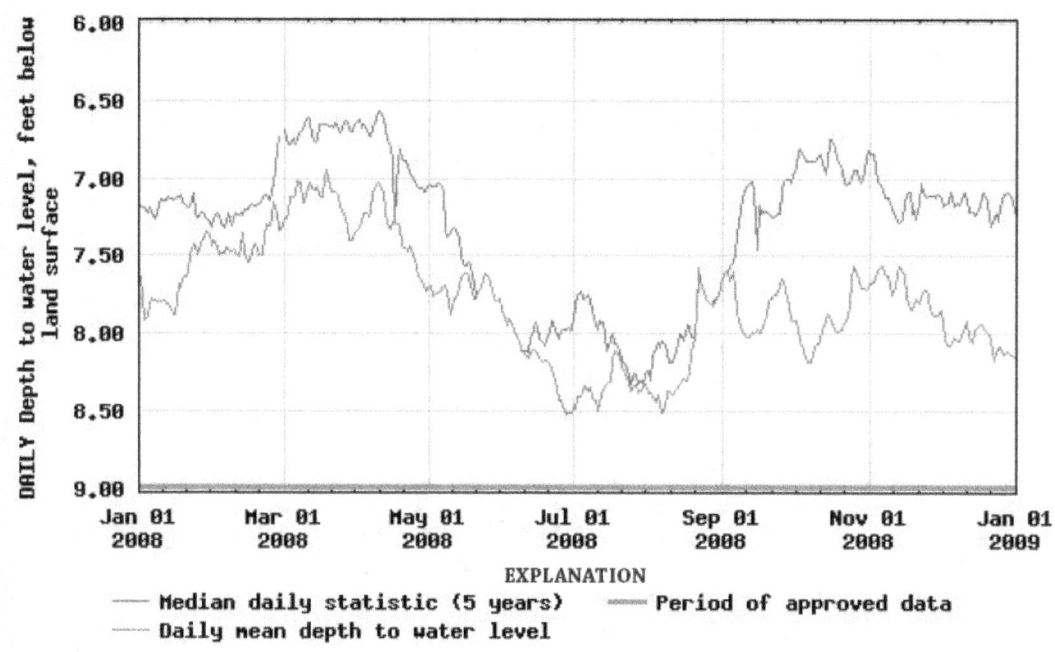

EXPLANATION
—— Median daily statistic (5 years)   ▬▬▬ Period of approved data
—— Daily mean depth to water level

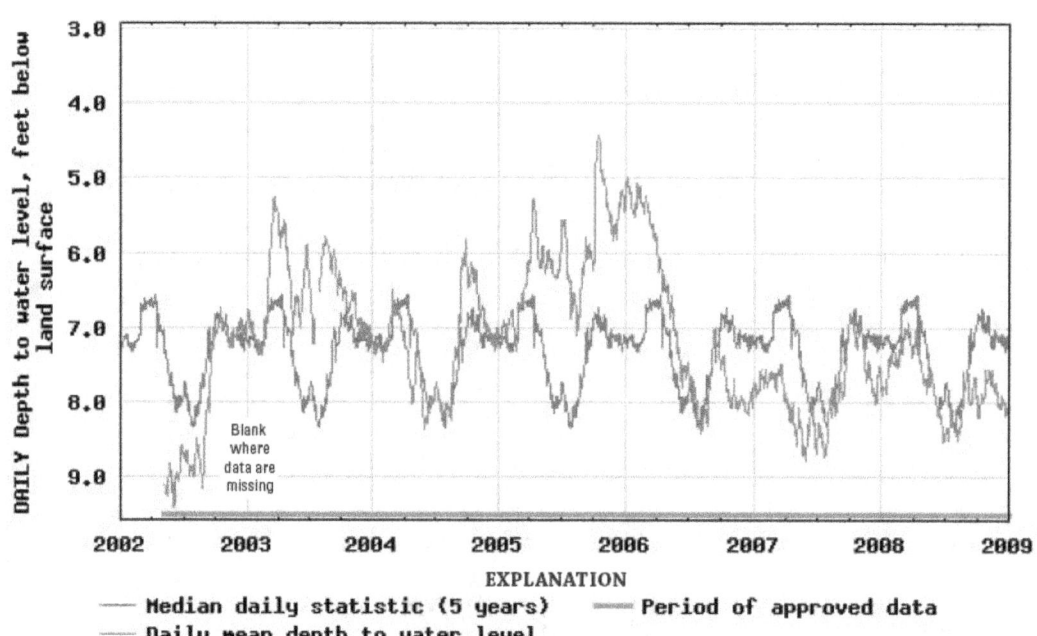

EXPLANATION
—— Median daily statistic (5 years)   ▬▬▬ Period of approved data
—— Daily mean depth to water level

Figure 7.   Periodic and daily mean water levels in well 34J082, surficial aquifer system, Glynn County, Georgia, 2002–2008.

Surficial aquifer system

310902081284201   Site Name: 34H515
Glynn County   Period of Record: 2005–2008
Well Depth: 200 feet   Datum: 9 feet NGVD 29   Well Diameter: 2.00 inches

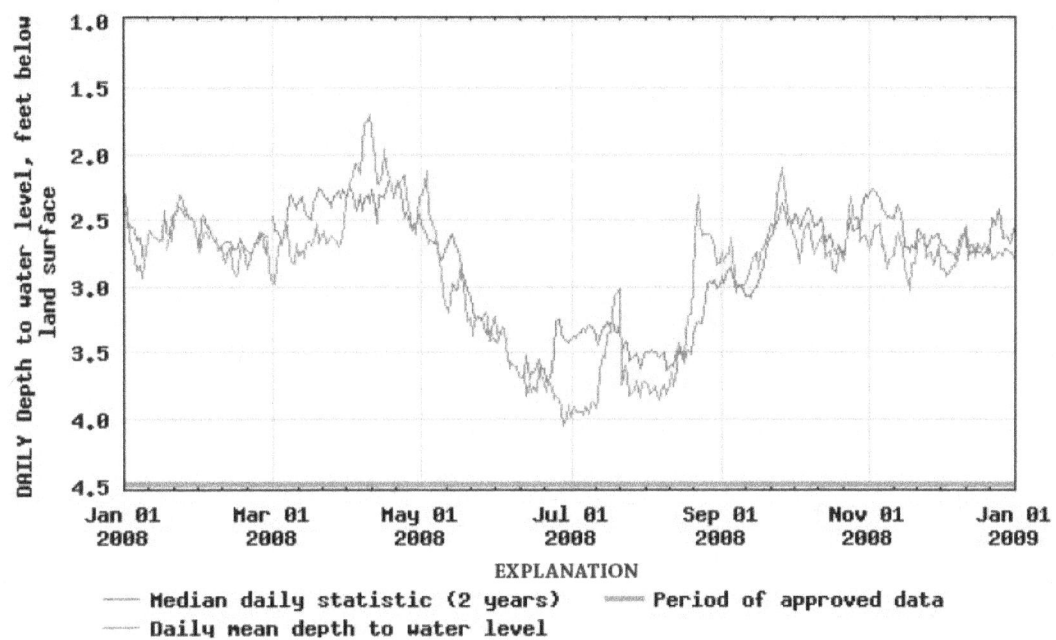

EXPLANATION

—— Median daily statistic (2 years)   ▬▬ Period of approved data
—— Daily mean depth to water level

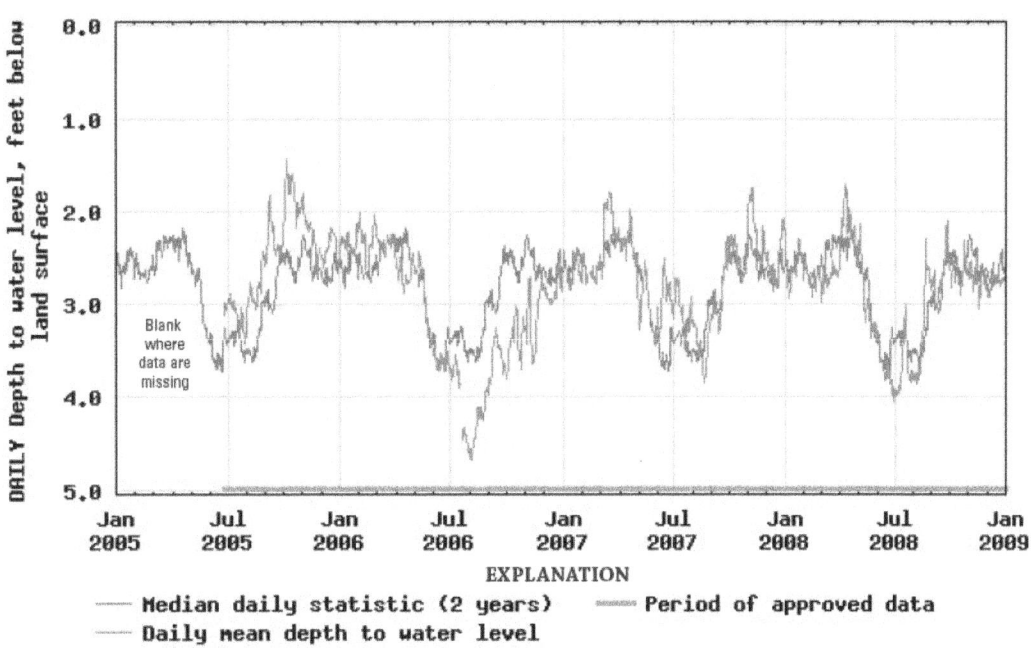

EXPLANATION

—— Median daily statistic (2 years)   ▬▬ Period of approved data
—— Daily mean depth to water level

Figure 8. Periodic and daily mean water levels in well 34H515, surficial aquifer system, Glynn County, Georgia, 2005–2008.

Brunswick Aquifer System

Water levels in the Brunswick aquifer system are monitored in four wells completed in the upper Brunswick aquifer and three wells completed in the lower Brunswick aquifer (table 1; fig. 9). Hydrographs for these wells are shown in figures 10–16. The water level in six of the wells was sufficient for comparison of percentiles and comparison to normal conditions. Well 35H077 has a 2-year period of record that is too short for comparison of percentiles and comparison to normal conditions. During 2008, water levels in five of the

seven wells were below the historical daily median for most of the year and approached or set new historic daily minimum values in wells 33J065 (fig. 11), 34J077 (fig. 12), 34J081 (fig. 13), and 34J080 (fig. 15). These declines correspond to a period of continued drought with below-normal precipitation from late 2005 through December 2008 (fig. 2). In well 34J077 (fig. 12) at the Golden Isles development, water levels also indicate the influence of pumping in that area. Since pumping from the Brunswick aquifer system at the Golden Isle production well began during 1999, the water level has dropped about 15 feet (ft).

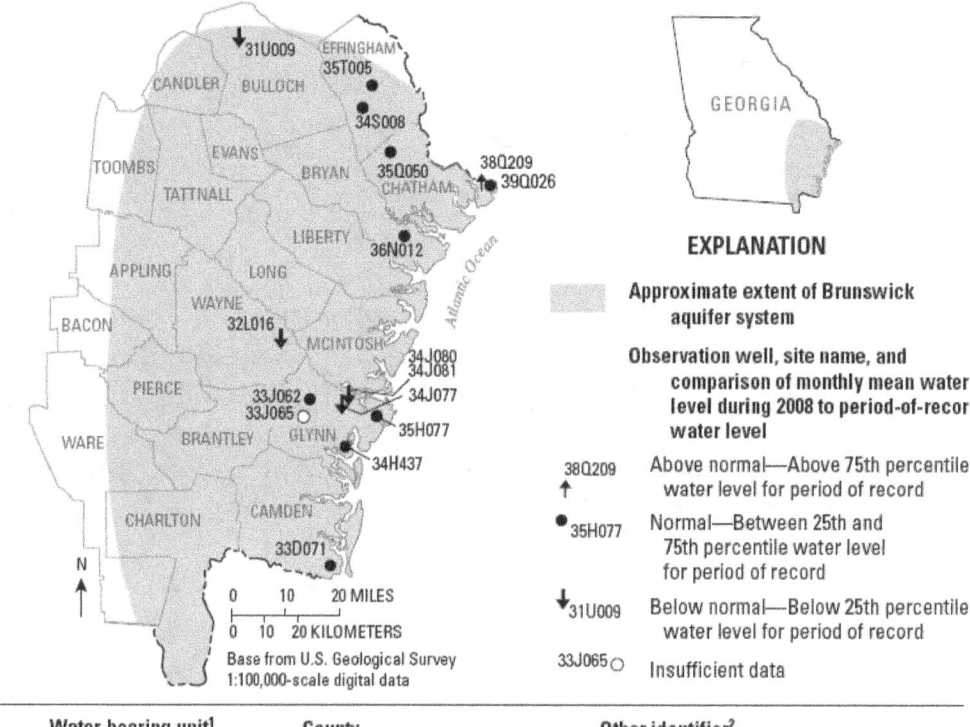

Site name	Water-bearing unit[1]	County	Other identifier[2]
36N012	L	Bryan	Genesis Pointe
31U009	UX	Bulloch	Georgia Geologic Survey, Hopeulikit, test well 2
33D071	U	Camden	Georgia Geologic Survey, St Marys, test well 2
35Q050	U	Chatham	Georgia Forestry Commission, test well CB-1
38Q209	B	Chatham	Fort Pulaski, Savannah Harbor Expansioin, monitoring well 3, COE
39Q026	UX	Chatham	Tybee Island, test well 3
34S008	LX	Effingham	Pineora test well EB-1
35T005	UX	Effingham	Springfield, Georgia, observation well
33J062	L	Glynn	Georgia Forestry Commission, test well GB-1
33J065	U	Glynn	Georgia Forestry Commission, test well GB-4
34H437	U	Glynn	Georgia Geologic Survey, Coffin Park, test well 2
34J077	U	Glynn	Golden Isle, test well 1S
35H077	L	Glynn	Coastal Sound Science Initiative, St. Simons test well 2
34J080	L	Glynn	Coastal Sound Science Initiative, Ebenezer Bend AR-2
34J081	U	Glynn	Coastal Sound Science Initiative, Ebenezer Bend AR-3
32L016	U	Wayne	Georgia Geologic Survey, Gardi, test well 2

[1]B, Brunswick aquifer system; L, lower Brunswick aquifer; U, upper Brunswick aquifer; UX, undifferentiated, low-permeability equivalent to the upper Brunswick aquifer; LX, undifferentiated, low-permeability equivalent to the lower Brunswick aquifer

[2]Georgia Geologic Survey now known as Georgia Environmental Protection Division

Figure 9.   Groundwater levels in the Brunswick aquifer system in the central and southern coastal areas, Georgia, 2008

Upper Brunswick aquifer

310901081284402   Site Name: 34H437
Glynn County   Period of Record: 1983–2008
Well Depth: 328 feet   Datum: 7.00 feet NGVD 29   Well Diameter: 10.00 inches

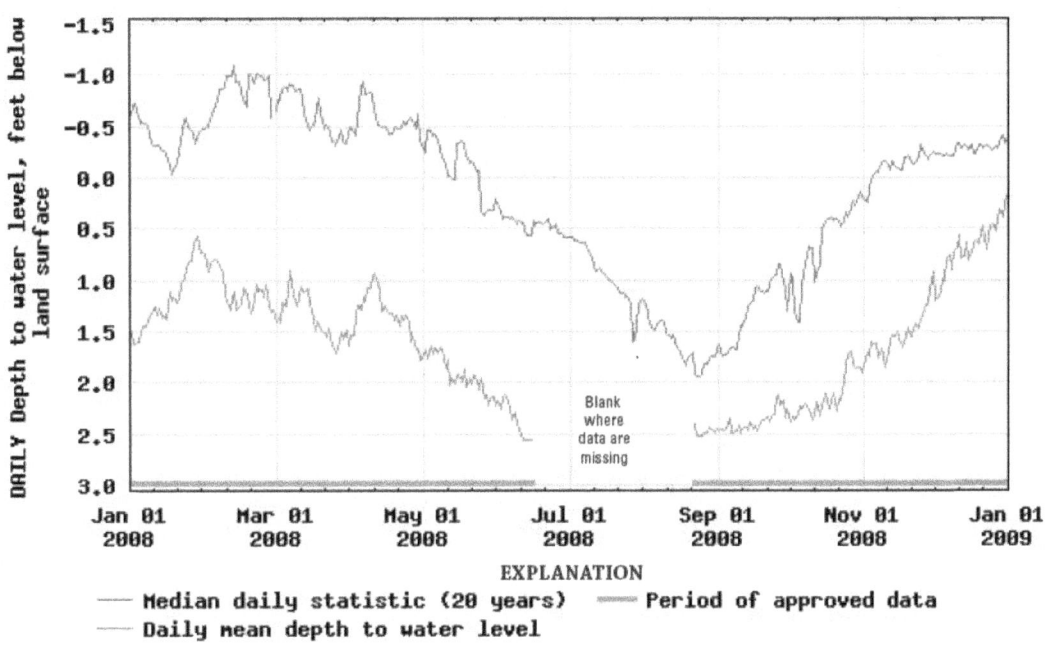

EXPLANATION
—— Median daily statistic (20 years)   ===== Period of approved data
—— Daily mean depth to water level

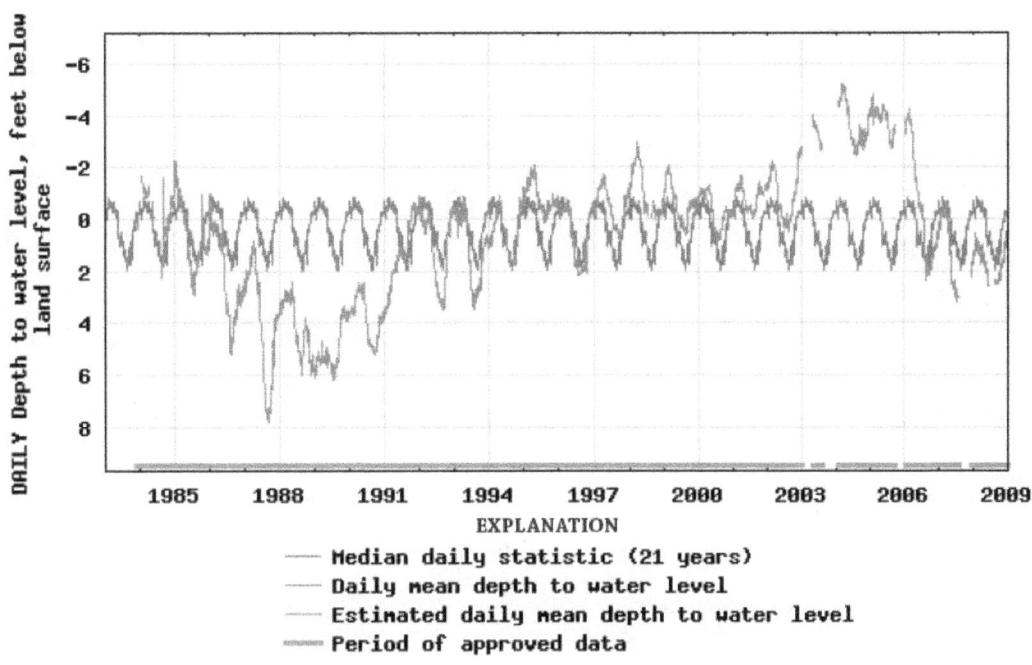

EXPLANATION
—— Median daily statistic (21 years)
—— Daily mean depth to water level
—— Estimated daily mean depth to water level
===== Period of approved data

Figure 10.   Periodic and daily mean water levels in well 34H437, upper Brunswick aquifer, Glynn County, Georgia, 1983–2008.

Upper Brunswick aquifer

311530081363904   Site Name: 33J065
Glynn County   Period of Record: 2001–2008
Well Depth: 412 feet   Datum: 12 feet NGVD 29   Well Diameter: 6.00 inches

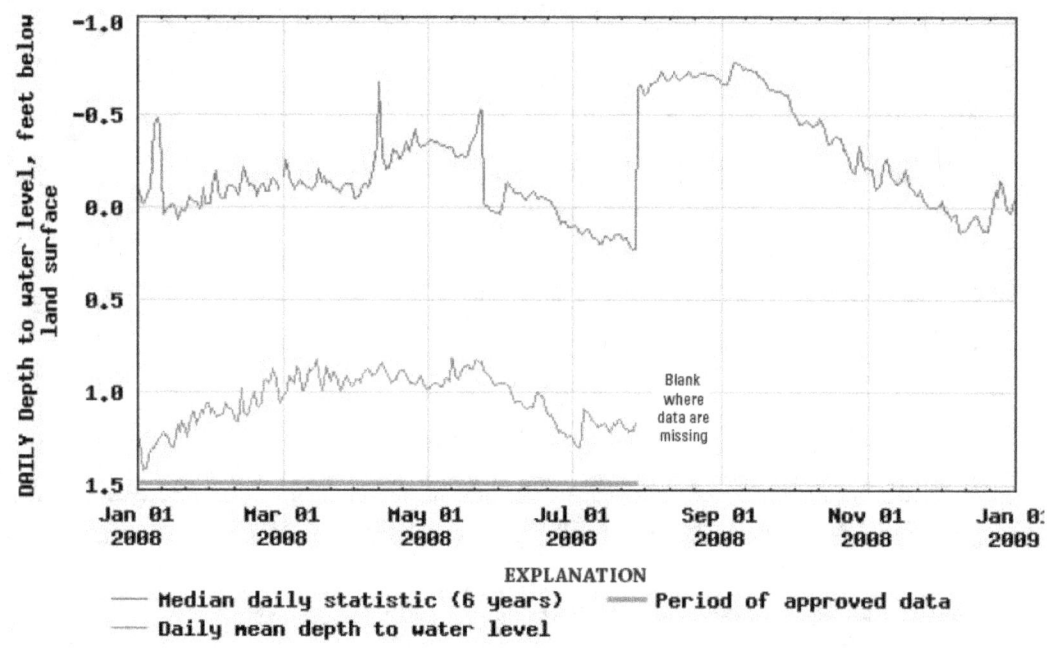

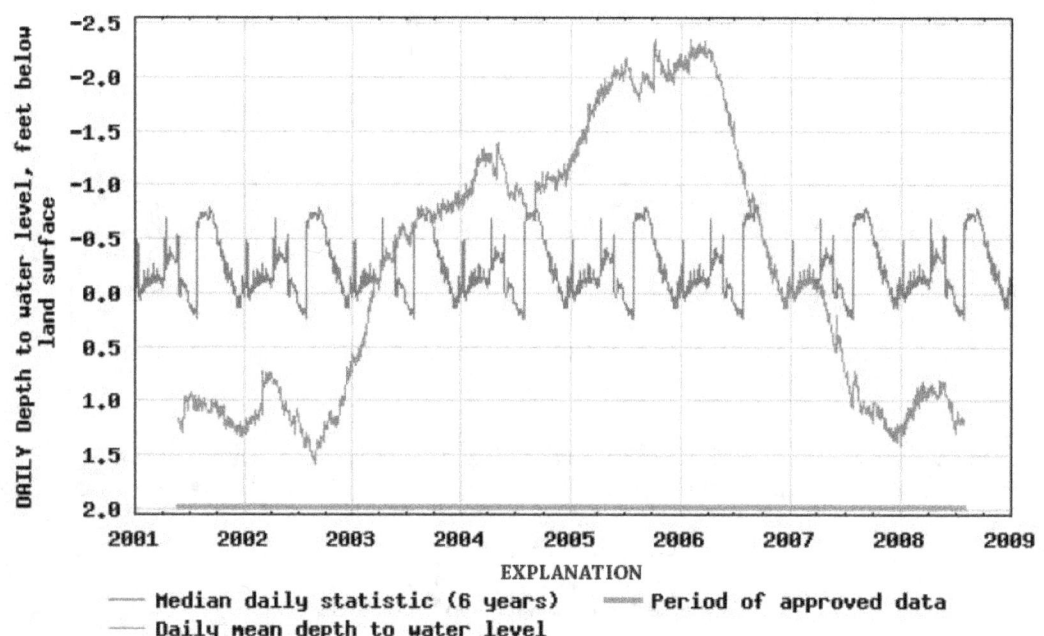

Figure 11.   Periodic and daily mean water levels in well 33J065 upper Brunswick aquifer, Glynn County, Georgia, 2001–2008

Upper Brunswick aquifer

311711081283002   Site Name: **34J077**
Glynn County   Period of Record: 1998–2008
Well Depth: 390 feet   Datum: 15 feet NGVD 29   Well Diameter: 4.00 inches

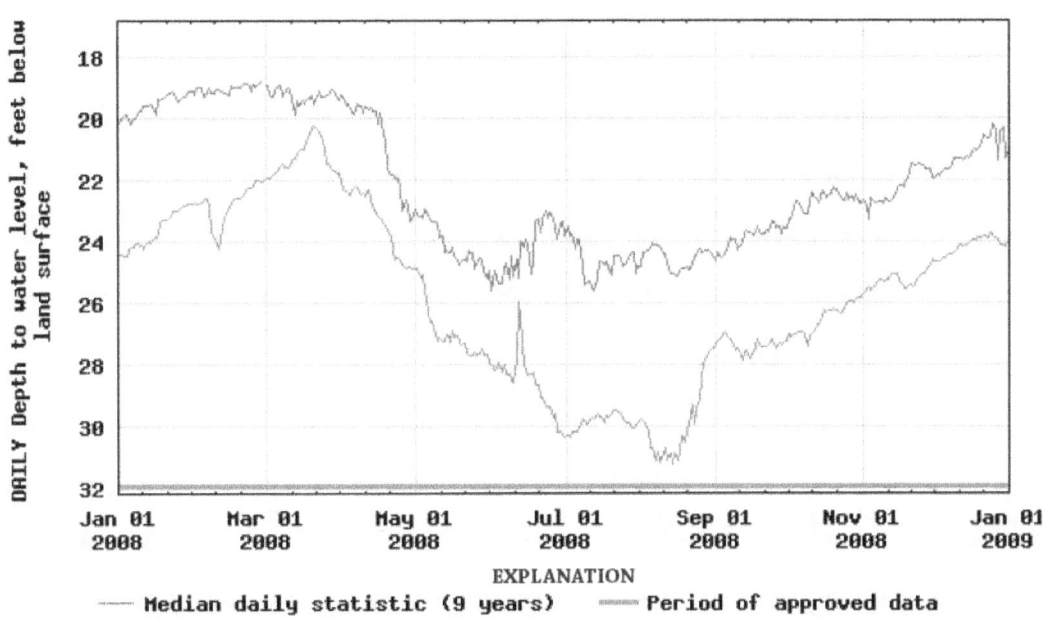

EXPLANATION
—— Median daily statistic (9 years)   ▭▭ Period of approved data
—— Daily mean depth to water level

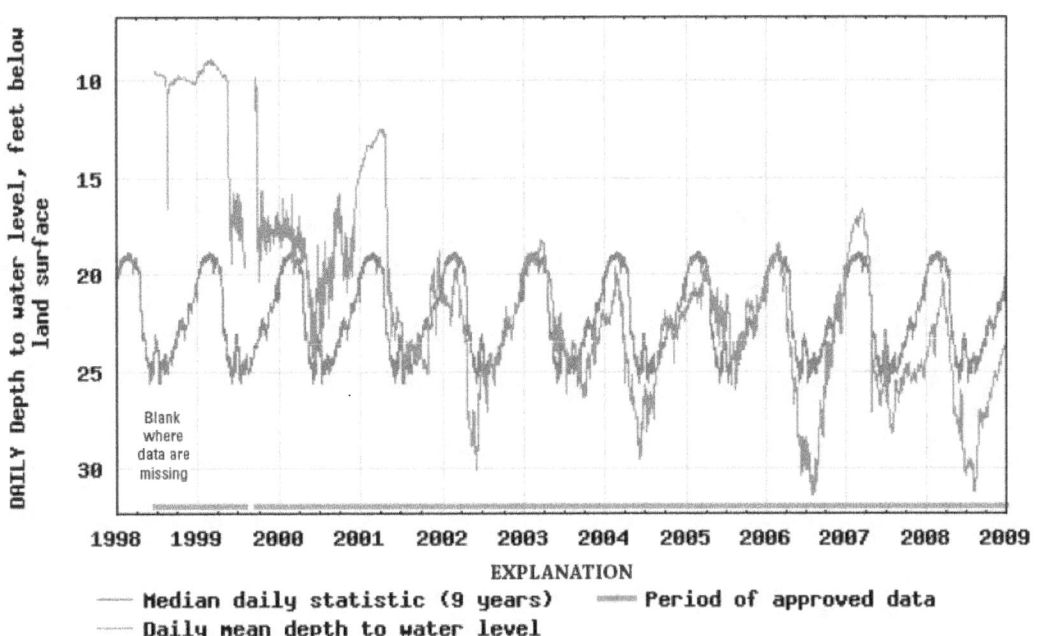

EXPLANATION
—— Median daily statistic (9 years)   ▭▭ Period of approved data
—— Daily mean depth to water level

Figure 12.   Periodic and daily mean water levels in well 34J077, upper Brunswick aquifer, Glynn County, Georgia 1998–2008

Upper Brunswick aquifer

311909081281102   Site Name: **34J081**
Glynn County   Period of Record: 2002–2008
Well Depth: 435 feet   Datum: 14.68 feet NGVD 29   Well Diameter: 4.00 inches

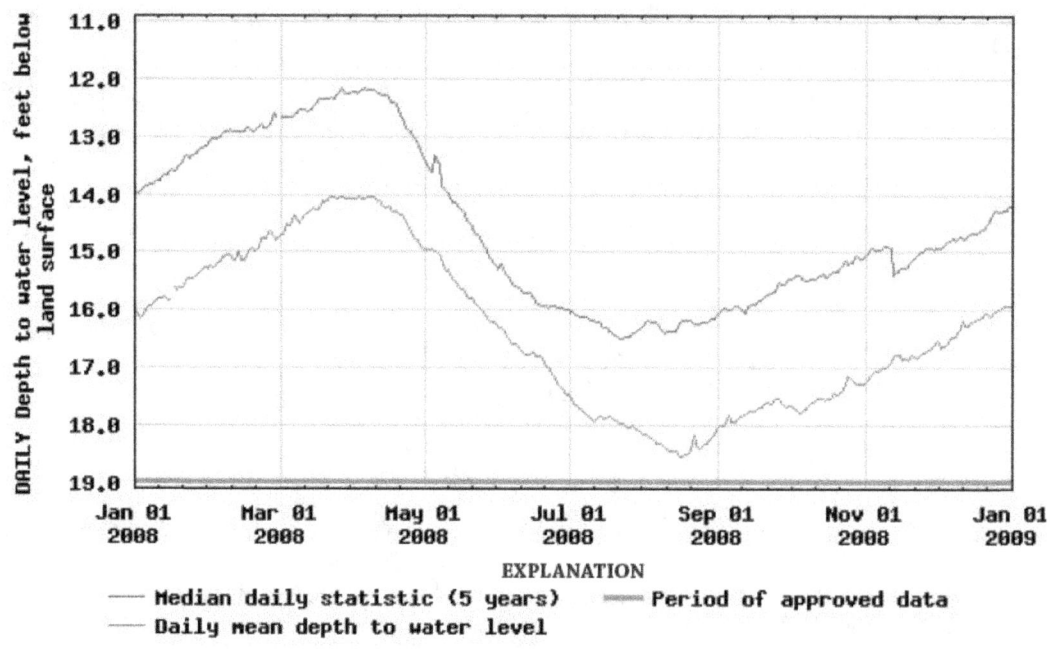

EXPLANATION
—— Median daily statistic (5 years)   ═══ Period of approved data
—— Daily mean depth to water level

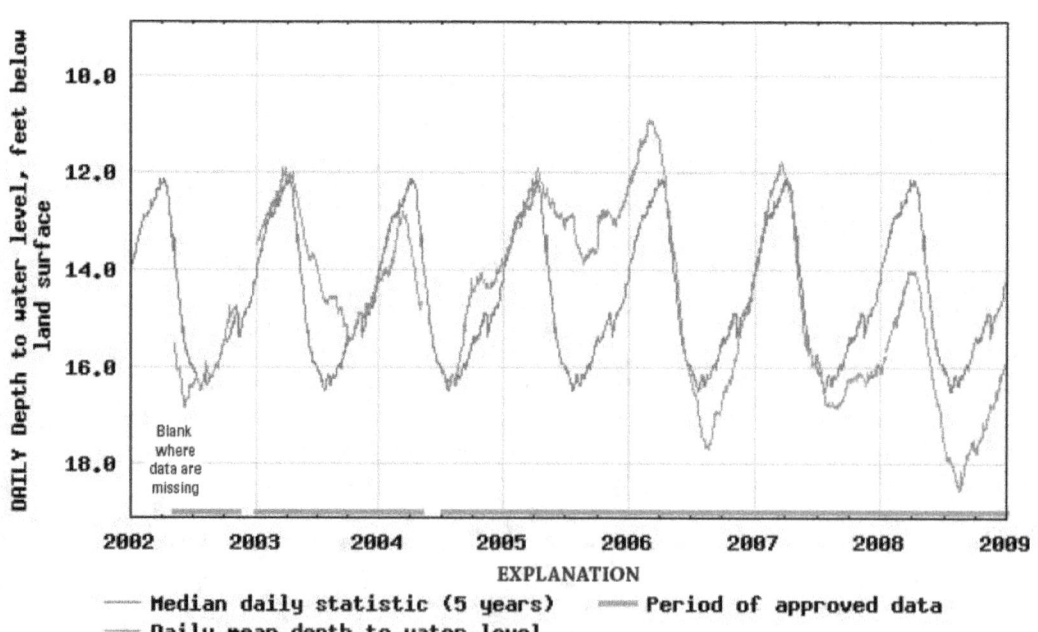

EXPLANATION
—— Median daily statistic (5 years)   ═══ Period of approved data
—— Daily mean depth to water level

Figure 13.   Periodic and daily mean water levels in well 34J081 upper Brunswick aquifer, Glynn County, Georgia, 2002–2008.

Lower Brunswick aquifer

311530081363901   Site Name: 33J062
Glynn County   Period of Record: 2001–2008
Well Depth: 500 feet   Datum: 12.00 feet NGVD 29   Well Diameter: 6.00 inches

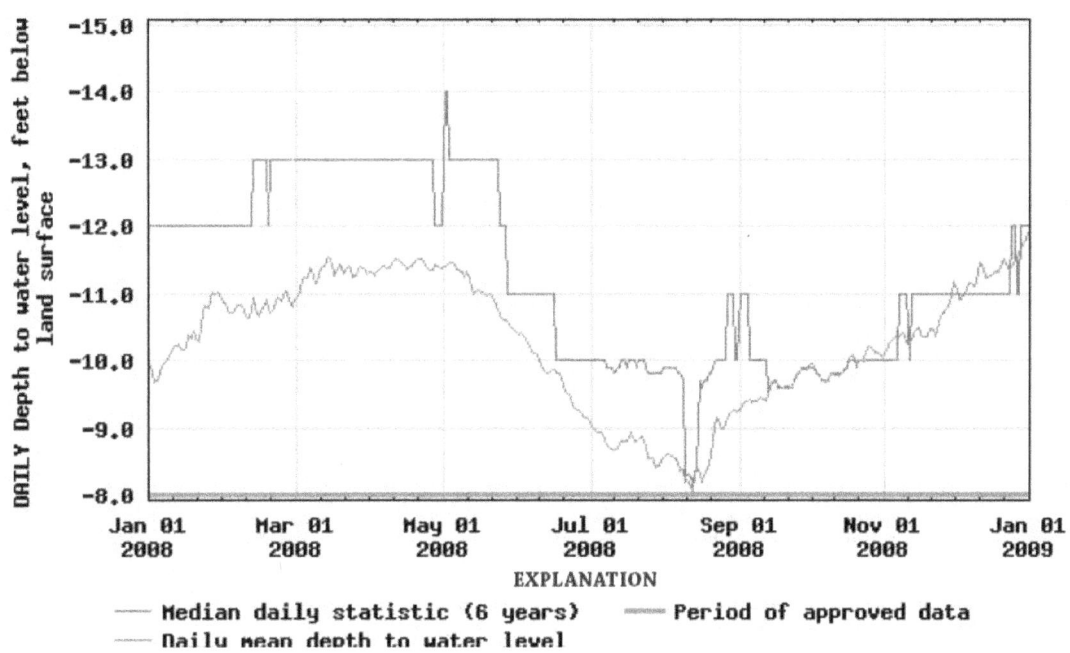

EXPLANATION

—— Median daily statistic (6 years)   ▬▬ Period of approved data
—— Daily mean depth to water level

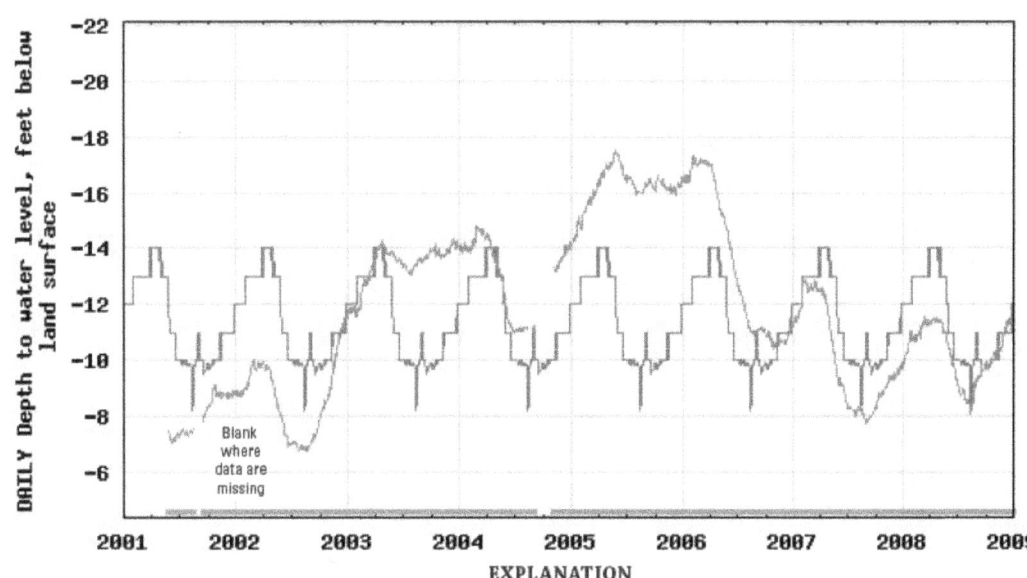

EXPLANATION

—— Median daily statistic (6 years)   ▬▬ Period of approved data
—— Daily mean depth to water level

Figure 14.   Periodic and daily mean water levels in well 33J062 lower Brunswick aquifer, Glynn County, Georgia, 2001–2008.

Lower Brunswick aquifer

311909081281101   Site Name: 34J080
Glynn County   Period of Record: 2002–2008
Well Depth: 555 feet   Datum: 13.66 feet NGVD 29   Well Diameter: 4.00 inches

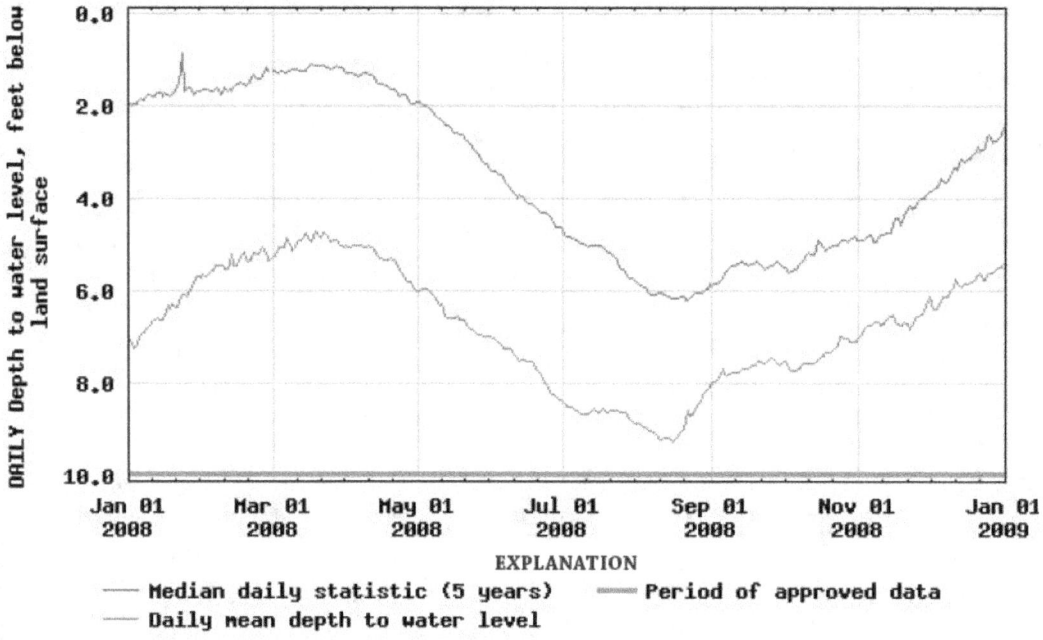

EXPLANATION

— Median daily statistic (5 years)   ▬▬ Period of approved data
— Daily mean depth to water level

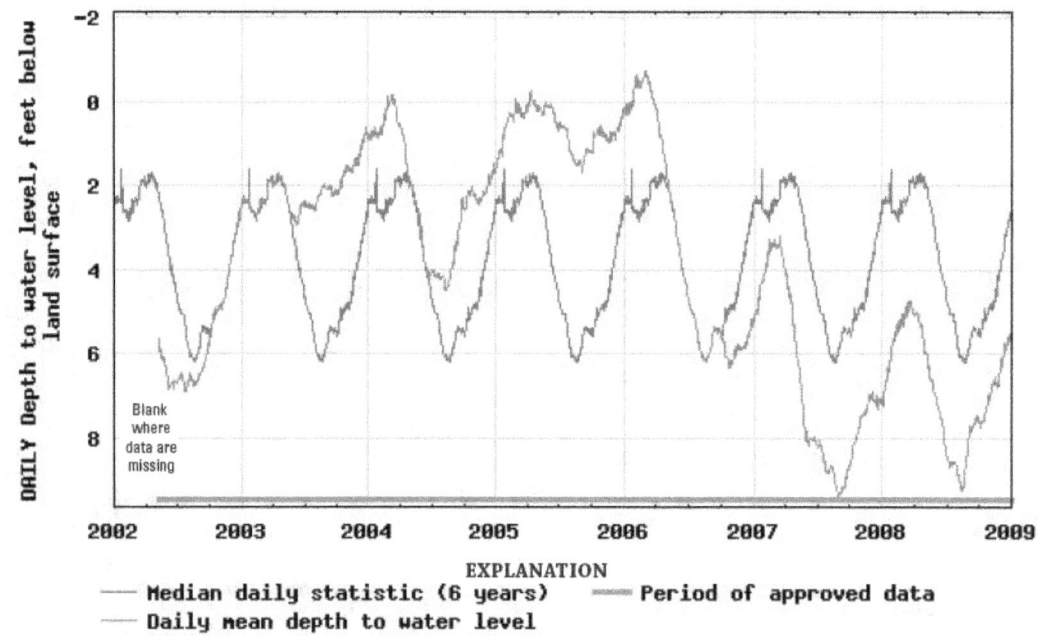

EXPLANATION

— Median daily statistic (6 years)   ▬▬ Period of approved data
— Daily mean depth to water level

Figure 15.   Periodic and daily mean water levels in well 34J080 lower Brunswick aquifer, Glynn County Georgia, 2002–2008.

Lower Brunswick aquifer

311456081210504   Site Name: 35H077
Glynn County   Period of Record: 2005–2008
Well Depth: 537 feet   Datum: 20 feet NGVD 29   Well Diameter: 6.00 inches

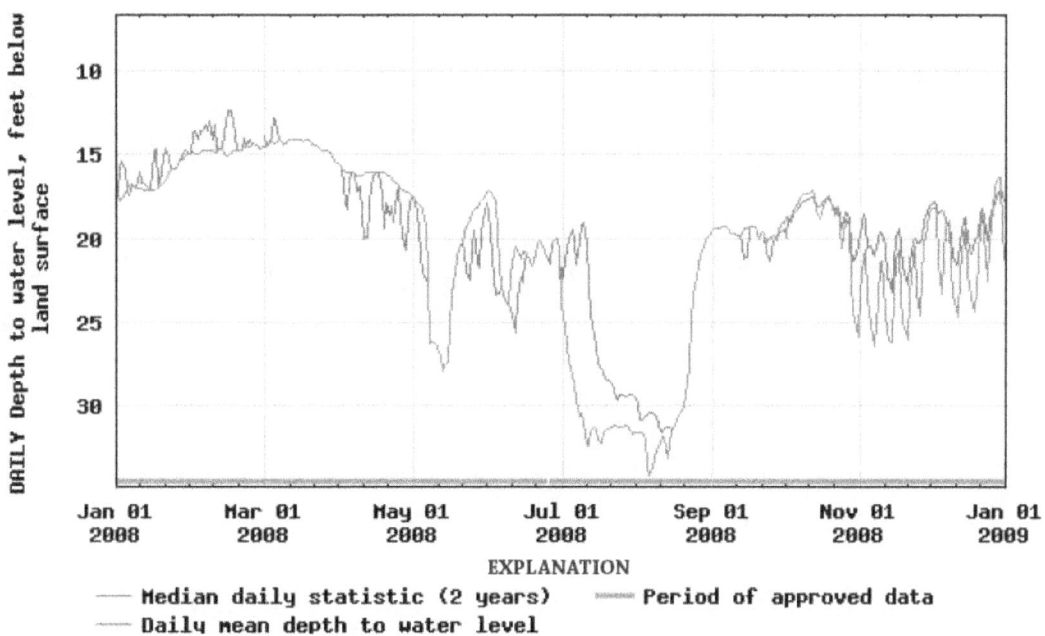

EXPLANATION

—— Median daily statistic (2 years)   ▒▒▒▒ Period of approved data
—— Daily mean depth to water level

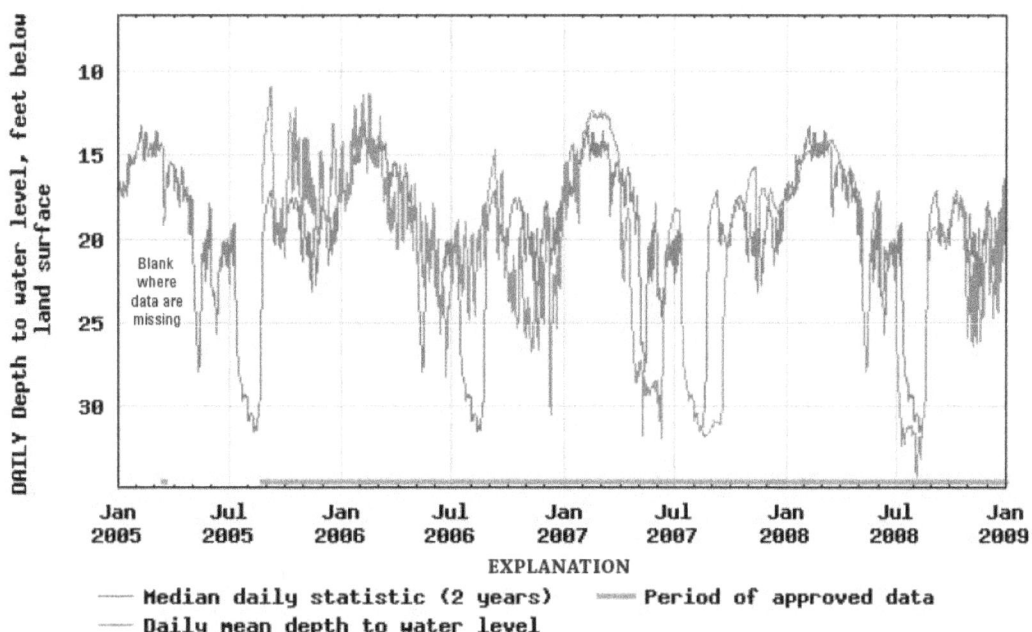

EXPLANATION

—— Median daily statistic (2 years)   ▒▒▒▒ Period of approved data
—— Daily mean depth to water level

Figure 16.   Periodic and daily mean water levels in well 35H077, lower Brunswick aquifer, Glynn County, Georgia 2005–2008.

Floridan Aquifer System

Water levels in the Floridan aquifer system in the Brunswick–Glynn County area are continuously monitored in 12 wells completed in the Upper Floridan aquifer (fig. 17; table 1) and in 7 wells completed in the Lower Floridan aquifer. Hydrographs for six of the Upper Floridan wells are shown in figures 18–23, and locations and hydrographs for seven Lower Floridan wells are shown in figures 24–31. The period of record was too short to display hydrographs for wells 35H070, 33H324, 33H325, 34H504, 34H505, and 34H514 (Upper Floridan aquifer) and 35H068 (Lower Floridan aquifer), which were installed in 2007 (fig. 1; table 1). Data for wells 33H324, 33H325, 34H504, 34H505, and 34H514 are included in the section on real-time groundwater monitoring stations.

Although not influenced directly by precipitation, water levels in the Floridan aquifer system generally declined during 2007–2008, corresponding to increased pumping demand. Despite this decline, water levels in 5 of the 12 wells completed in the Upper Floridan aquifer were at or above historical daily median levels during most of 2008, reflecting the continuing effect of pumping reductions in the coastal area since the 1990s (wells 33H133, 33H207, 33H127, 34H334, and 34H371). The period of record is too short to allow for statistical comparisons for six Upper Floridan aquifer wells (33H324, 33H325, 34H504, 34H505, 34G033, and 35H070).

In addition to continuous recorders, synoptic water-level measurements were collected in 21 wells completed in the Upper Floridan aquifer during July 2008, and a potentiometric-surface map was prepared using 19 of the water-level measurements (fig. 17). The map indicates that the principal directions of groundwater flow during 2008 remained from south to north and from east to west, following the gradient created by large industrial withdrawals in the northern and western parts of the Brunswick area (fig. 17).

Water levels in the Lower Floridan aquifer also declined during 2007 and 2008 in response to increased pumping (fig. 24). Water levels in five of the eight wells (33H188, 33H206, 33J044, 34H391, and 34H436) were at or below historical daily median levels during most of the year.

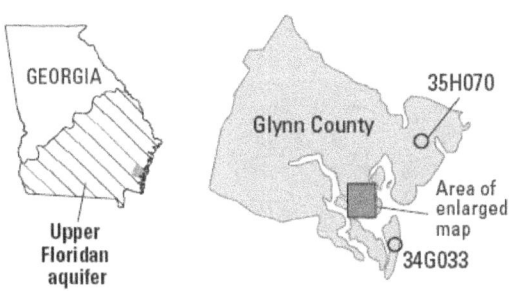

Site name	County	Other identifier[1]
33H127	Glynn	U.S. Geological Survey, test well 3
33H133	Glynn	U.S. Geological Survey, test well 6
33H207	Glynn	Georgia-Pacific, south test well 2
33H324	Glynn	Georgia-Pacific, Lower water-bearing zone Coastal Sound Science Initiative
33H325	Glynn	Georgia-Pacific, Upper water-bearing zone Coastal Sound Science Initiative
34G033	Glynn	Jekyll Island No. 9
34H334	Glynn	U.S. Geological Survey, test well 4
34H371	Glynn	U.S. Geological Survey, test well 11
34H504	Glynn	Southside Baptist Church
34H505	Glynn	Southside Baptist Church
34H514	Glynn	City of Brunswick, Perry Park
35H070	Glynn	GGS, St. Simons Upper Floridan

[1]Georgia Geologic Survey (GGS) now known as Georgia Environmental Protection Division

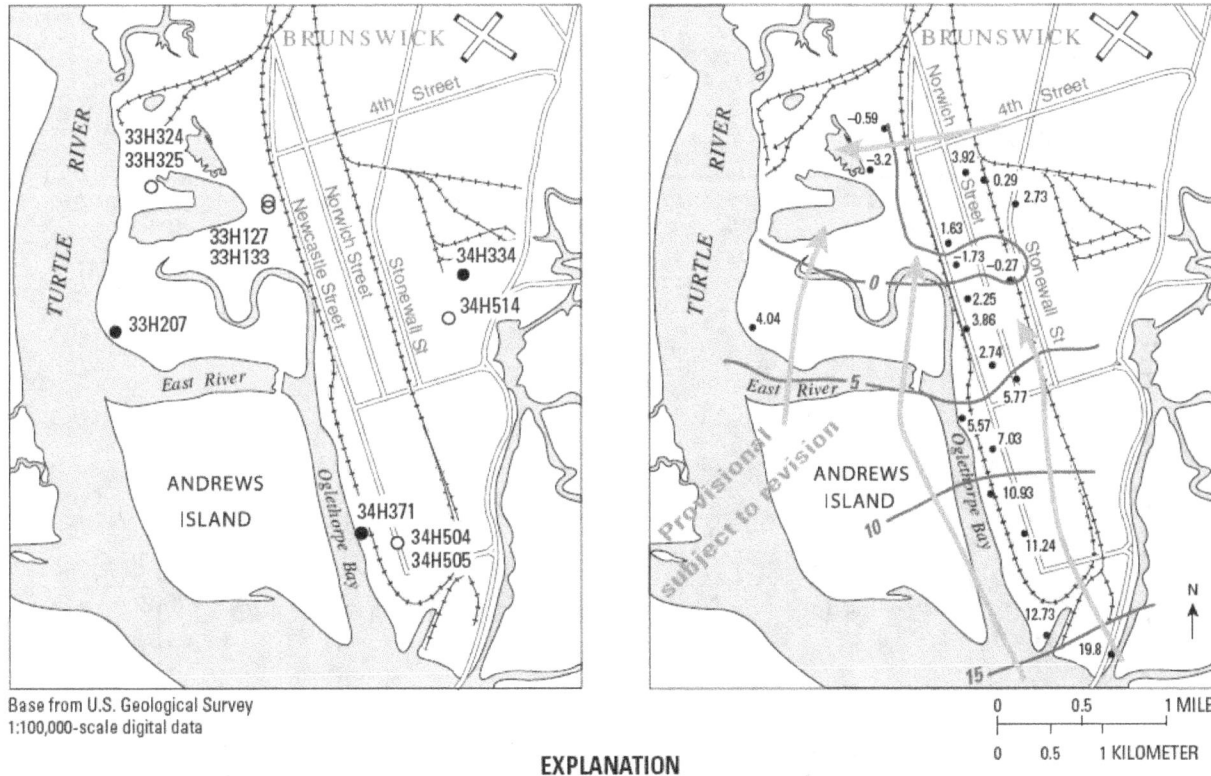

Base from U.S. Geological Survey
1:100,000-scale digital data

EXPLANATION

Observation well, site name, and comparison of mean annual water level during 2008 to period-of-record water level

● 33H207 Normal—Between 25th and 75th percentile water level for period of record

○ 33H325 No data or insufficient data

—— *15* —— **Potentiometric contour**—Shows altitude at which water level would have stood in tightly cased wells in the Upper Floridan aquifer, July 2008. Contour interval 5 feet. Datum is NAVD 88

⇨ **General direction of groundwater flow**

Figure 17. Groundwater level monitoring network and potentiometric surfaces for the Upper Floridan aquifer in the Brunswick–Glynn County area, July 2008.

Upper Floridan aquifer

311007081301702   **Site Name: 33H133**
Glynn County   Period of Record: 1964–2008
Well Depth: 790 feet   Datum: 6.71 feet NGVD 29   Well Diameter: 4.00 inches

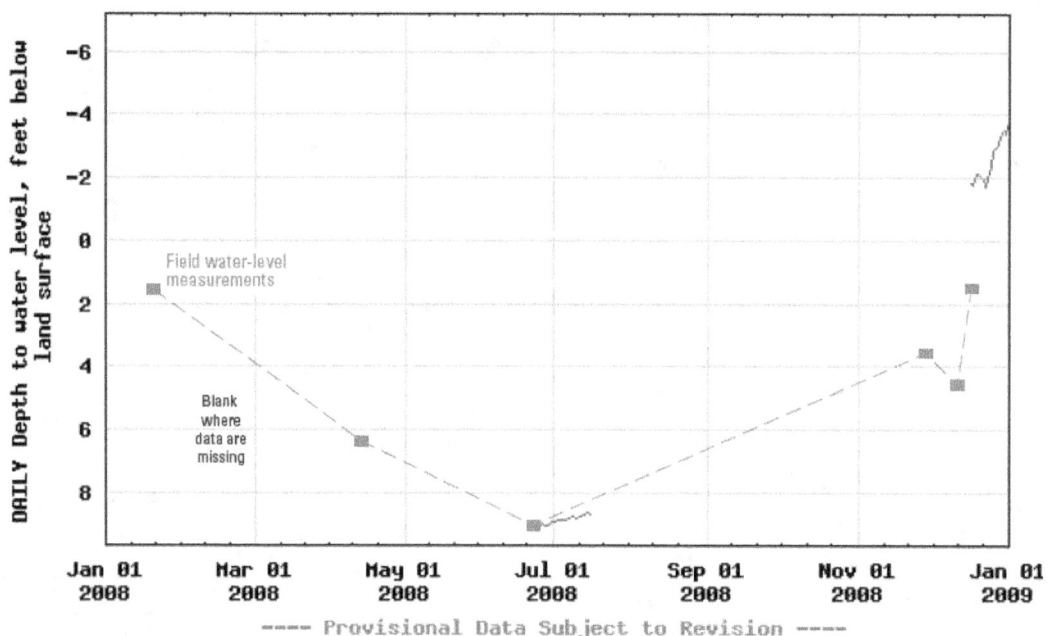

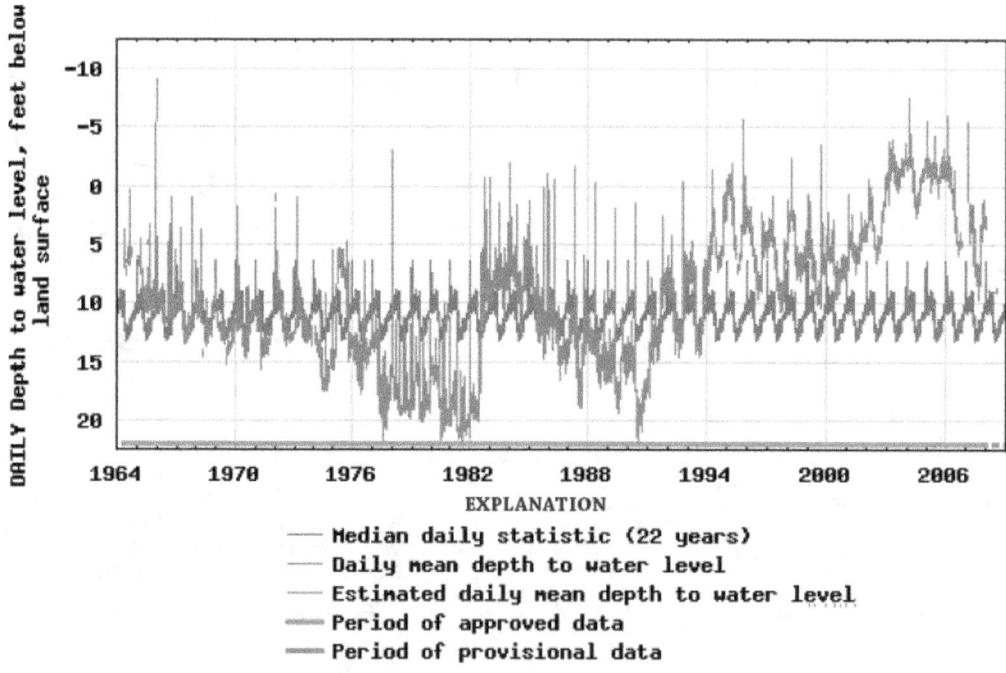

EXPLANATION

——— Median daily statistic (22 years)
——— Daily mean depth to water level
——— Estimated daily mean depth to water level
▬▬▬ Period of approved data
▬▬▬ Period of provisional data

Figure 18.   Periodic and daily mean water levels in well 33H133, Upper Floridan aquifer, Glynn County, Georgia, 1964–2008.

Upper Floridan aquifer

310925081312202

Glynn County

Well Depth: 720 feet   Datum: 7.00 feet NGVD 29

Site Name: **33H207**

Period of Record: 1983–2008

Well Diameter: 4.00 inches

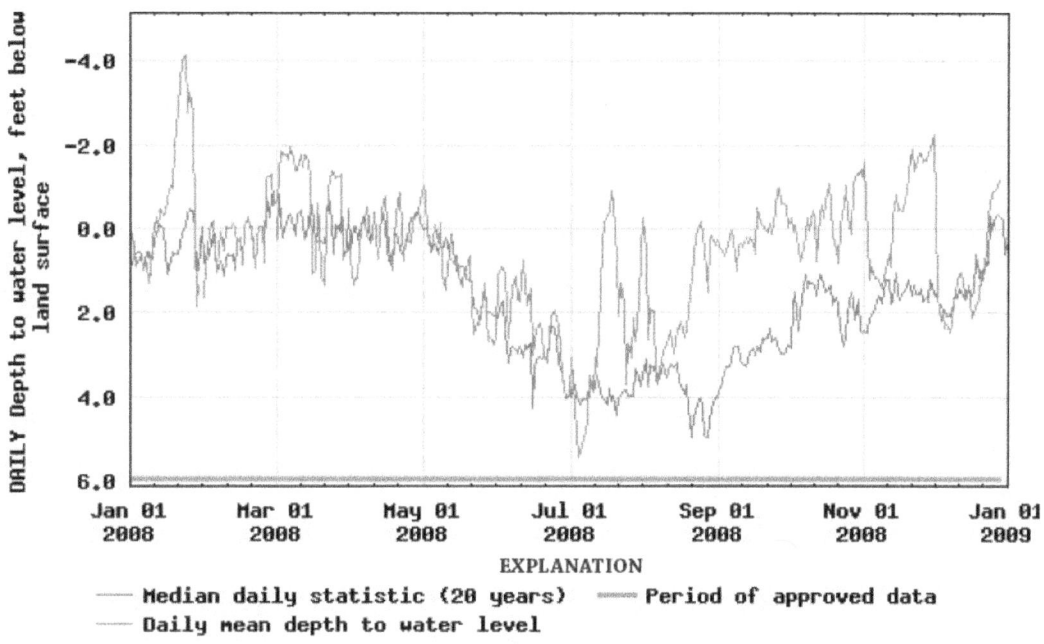

EXPLANATION

—— Median daily statistic (20 years)   ——— Period of approved data

—— Daily mean depth to water level

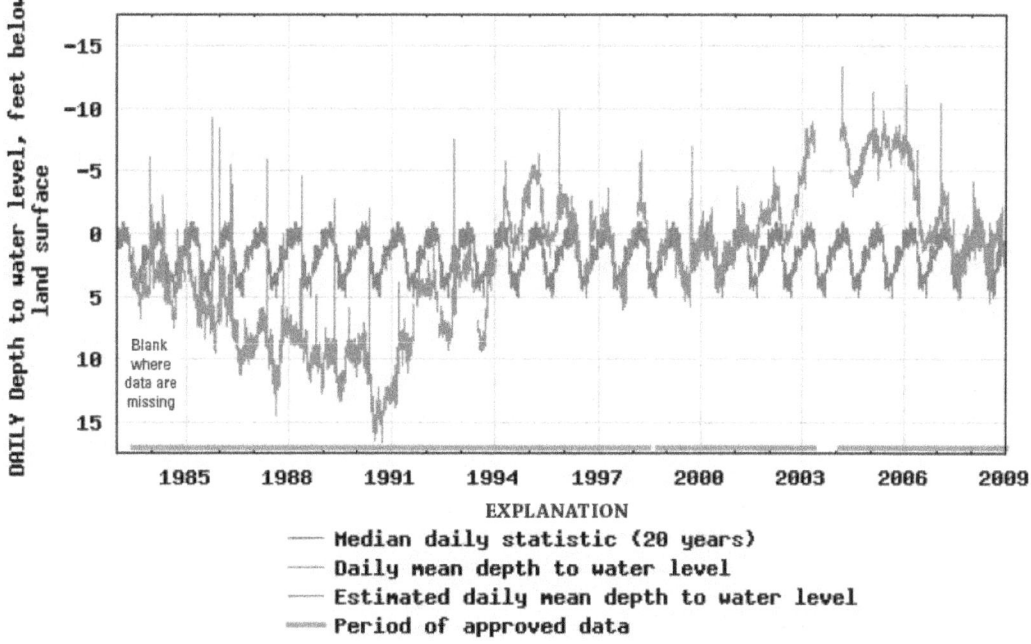

EXPLANATION

—— Median daily statistic (20 years)

—— Daily mean depth to water level

—— Estimated daily mean depth to water level

——— Period of approved data

Figure 19   Periodic and daily mean water levels in well 33H207, Upper Floridan aquifer, Glynn County Georgia 1983–2008.

Upper Floridan aquifer

310418081244701   **Site Name: 34G033**
Glynn County   Period of Record: 2004–2008
Well Depth: 751 feet Datum: 13.00 feet NGVD 29 Well Diameter: 8.00 inches

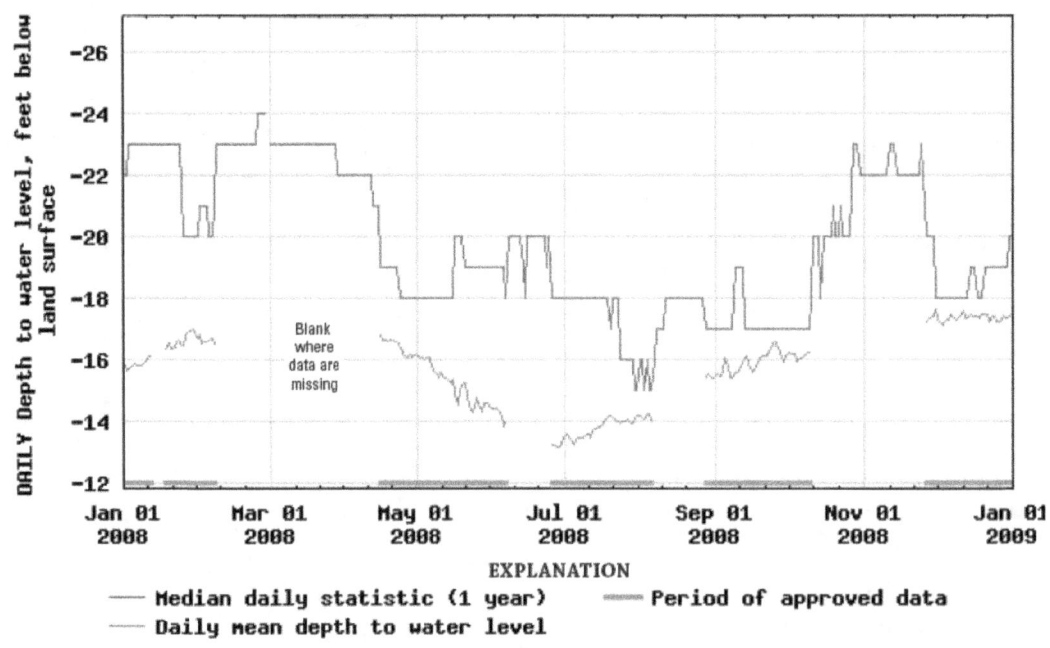

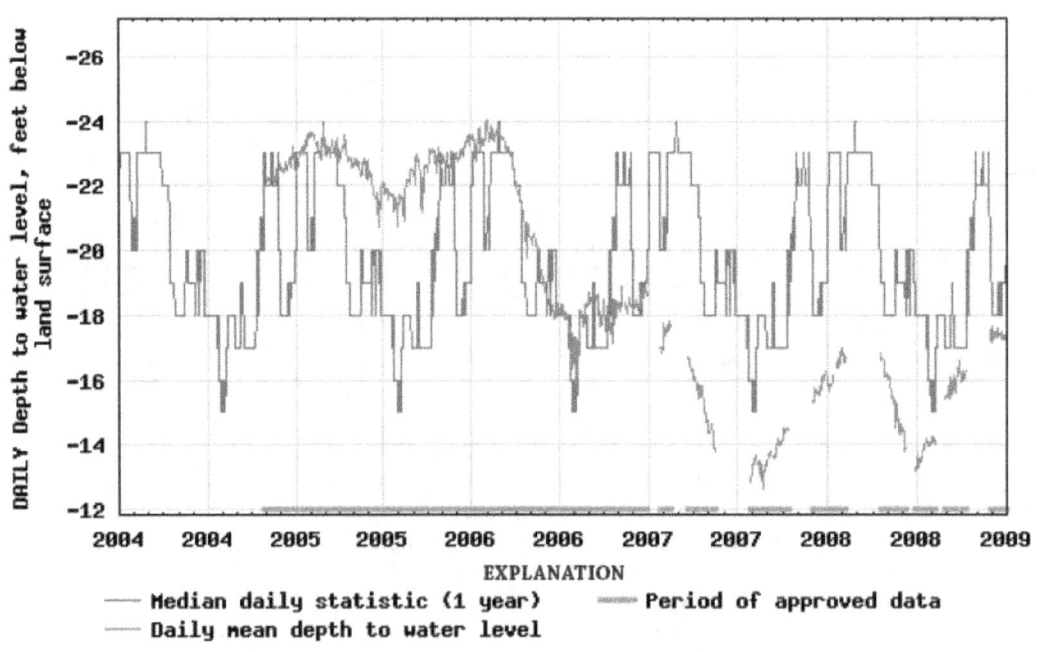

Figure 20.   Periodic and daily mean water levels in well 34G033, Upper Floridan aquifer, Glynn County, Georgia, 2004–2008.

Upper Floridan aquifer

311007081301701   **Site Name: 33H127**

Glynn County   Period of Record: 1962–2008

Well Depth: 952 feet   Datum: 6.15 feet NGVD 29   Well Diameter: 7.00 inches

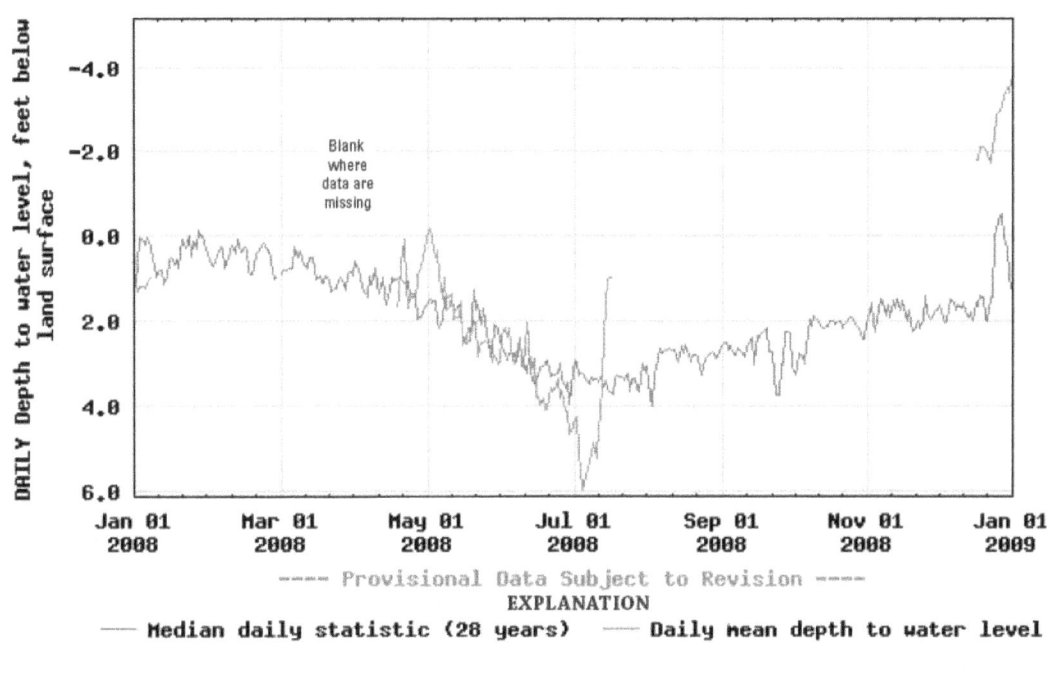

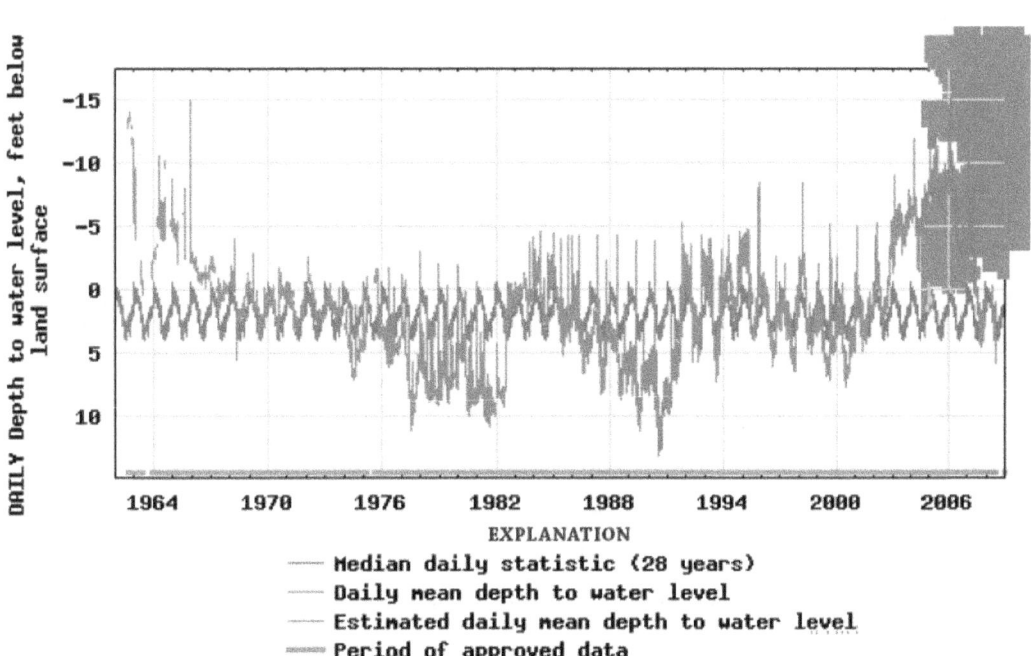

Figure 21   Periodic and daily mean water levels in well 33H127, Upper Floridan aquifer, Glynn County, Georgia, 1962–2008.

Upper Floridan aquifer

310938081285301   **Site Name: 34H334**
Glynn County   Period of Record: 1962–2008
Well Depth: 980 feet   Datum: 8.33 feet NGVD 29   Well Diameter: 4.00 inches

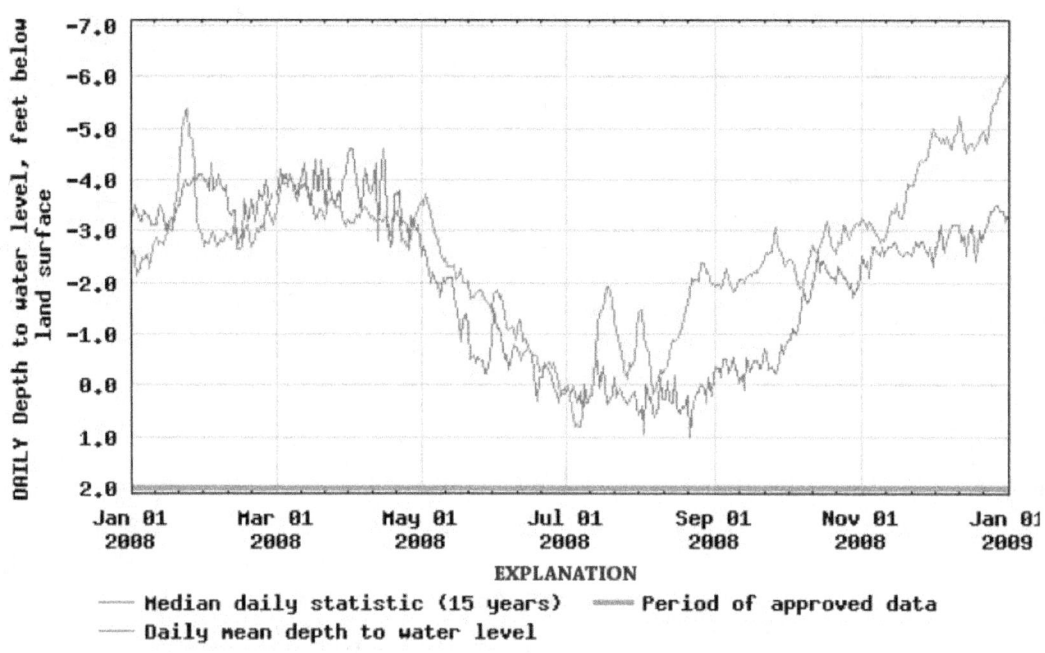

EXPLANATION
—— Median daily statistic (15 years)   ≡≡≡ Period of approved data
—— Daily mean depth to water level

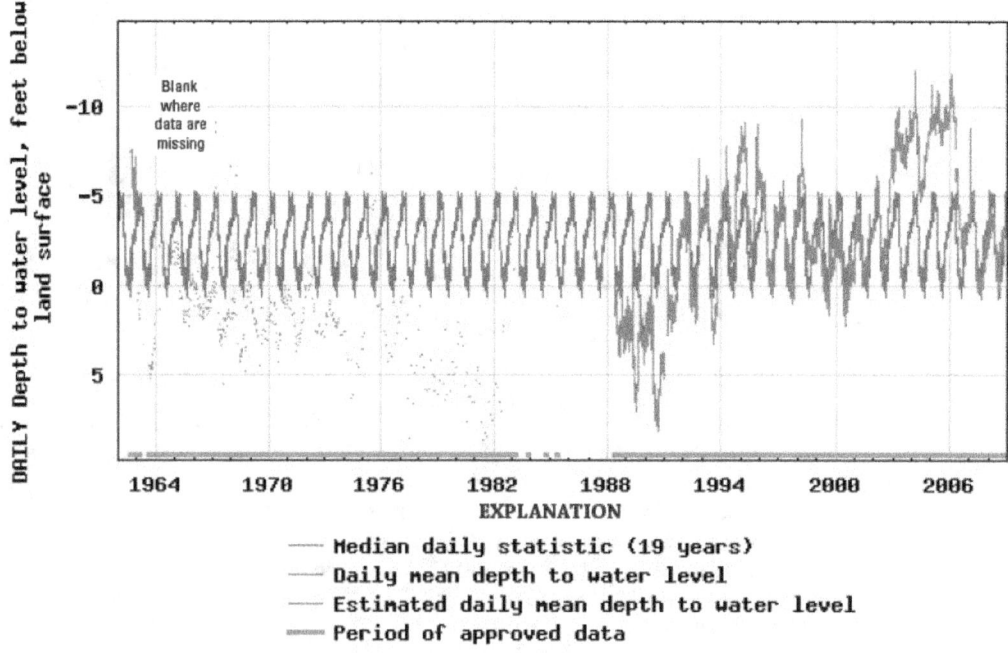

EXPLANATION
—— Median daily statistic (19 years)
—— Daily mean depth to water level
—— Estimated daily mean depth to water level
≡≡≡ Period of approved data

Figure 22.   Periodic and daily mean water levels in well 34H334, Upper Floridan aquifer, Glynn County, Georgia, 1962–2008.

Upper Floridan aquifer

310818081293701   Site Name: **34H371**
Glynn County   Period of Record: 1967–2008
Well Depth: 700 feet   Datum: 9.49 feet NGVD 29   Well Diameter: 2.00 inches

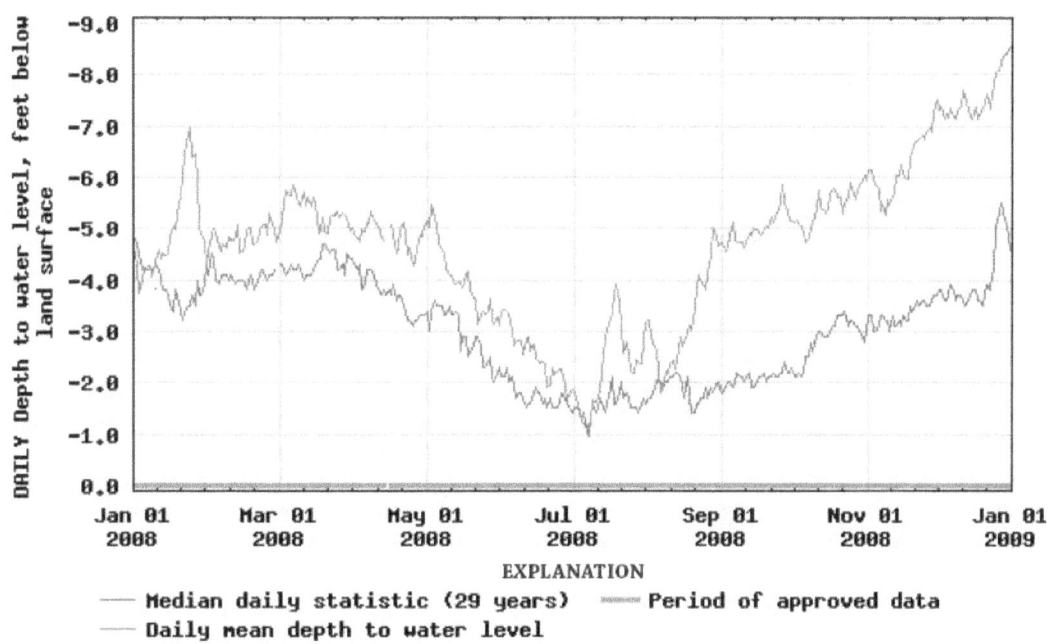

EXPLANATION
— Median daily statistic (29 years)   ⸺ Period of approved data
— Daily mean depth to water level

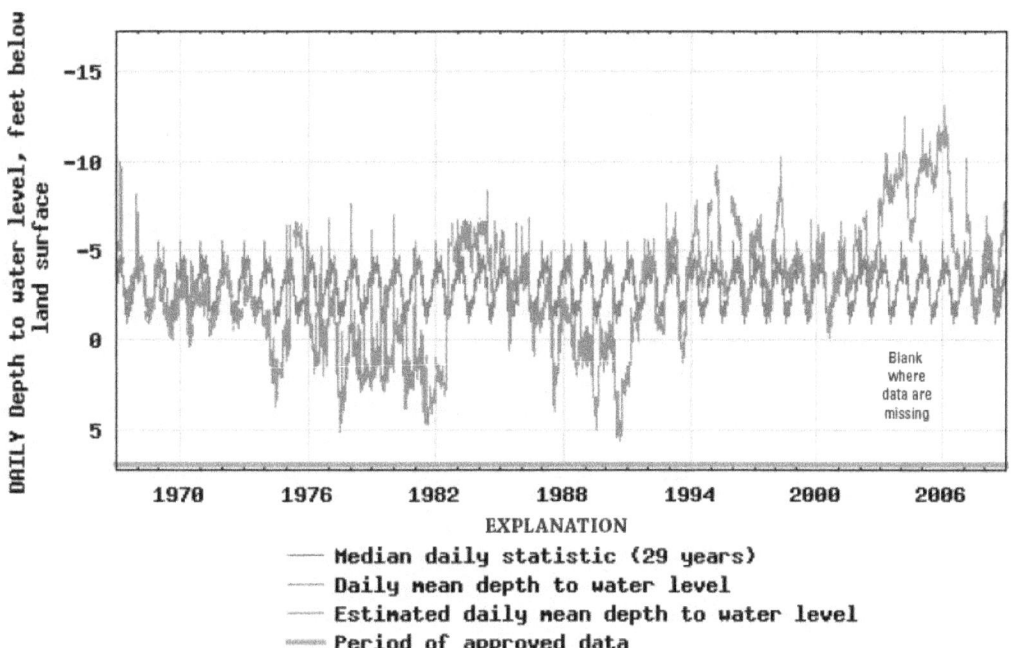

EXPLANATION
— Median daily statistic (29 years)
— Daily mean depth to water level
— Estimated daily mean depth to water level
⸺ Period of approved data

Figure 23.   Periodic and daily mean water levels in well 34H371 Upper Floridan aquifer, Glynn County, Georgia, 1967–2008

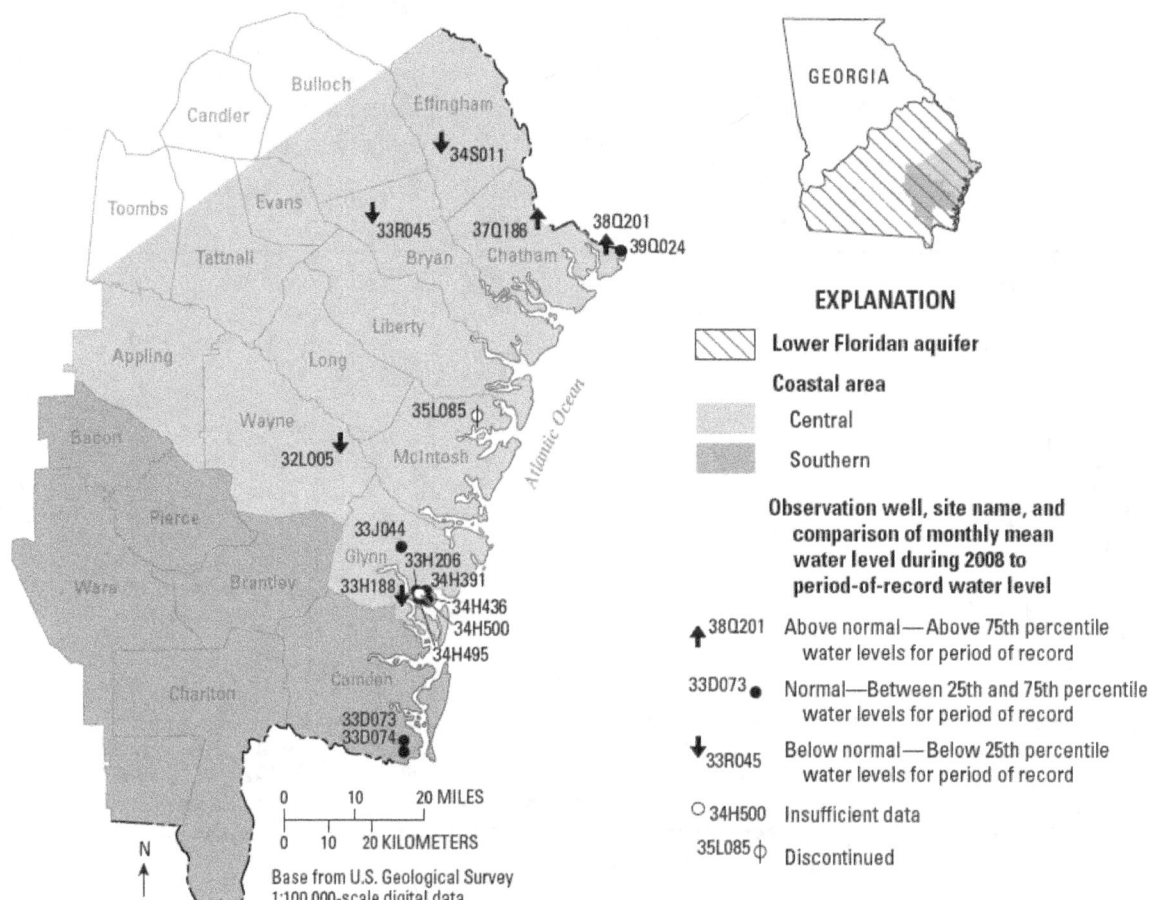

Site name	Water-bearing unit[1]	County	Other identifier[2]
33R045	LF	Bryan	Coastal Sound Science Initiative test well
33D073	LF	Camden	St Marys, test well (deep)
33D074	LF	Camden	Coastal Sound Science Initiative, St Marys test well 2
37Q186	P	Chatham	Hutchinson Island, test well 2
38Q201	P	Chatham	Georgia Geologic Survey, Fort Pulaski, test well
39Q024	LF	Chatham	Georgia Geologic Survey, Tybee Island, test well 1
34S011	LF	Effingham	Coastal Sound Science Initiative, Pineora Ball Park test well
33H188	F	Glynn	U.S. Geological Survey, test well 26
33H206	LF	Glynn	Georgia-Pacific, south, test well 1
33J044	LF	Glynn	U.S. Geological Survey, test well 27
34H391	LF	Glynn	U.S. Geological Survey, test well 16
34H436	LF	Glynn	Georgia Geologic Survey, Coffin Park, test well 1
34H495	F	Glynn	U.S. Geological Survey, test well 29
34H500	LF	Glynn	U.S. Geological Survey, test well 30
35L085	LF	McIntosh	Hawthorne, test well 1
32L005	LF	Wayne	Hopkins No. 2

[1]LF, Lower Floridan aquifer; P, Paleocene unit of lower permeability; F, Fernandina permeable zone (part of Lower Floridan aquifer)
[2]Georgia Geologic Survey now known as Georgia Environmental Protection Division

Figure 24.   Groundwater levels in the Lower Floridan aquifer in the central and southern coastal areas, Georgia, 2008.

Lower Floridan aquifer

310810081323501   **Site Name: 33H188**
Glynn County   Period of Record: 1978–2008
Well Depth: 2,720 feet Datum: 9.37 feet NGVD 29 Well Diameter: 10.00 inches

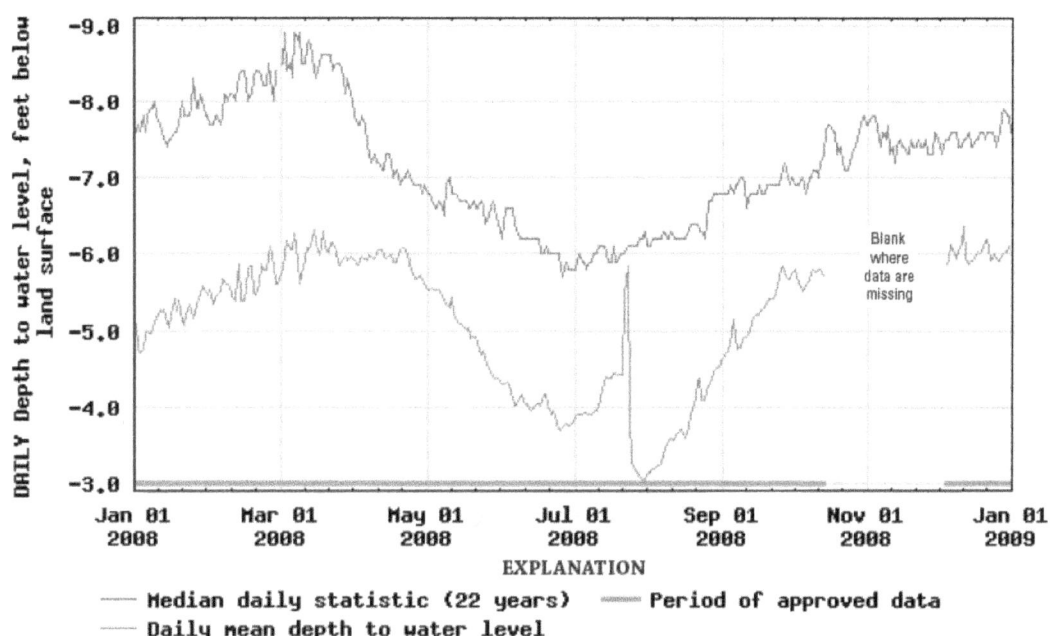

EXPLANATION

—— Median daily statistic (22 years)   ▬▬ Period of approved data
—— Daily mean depth to water level

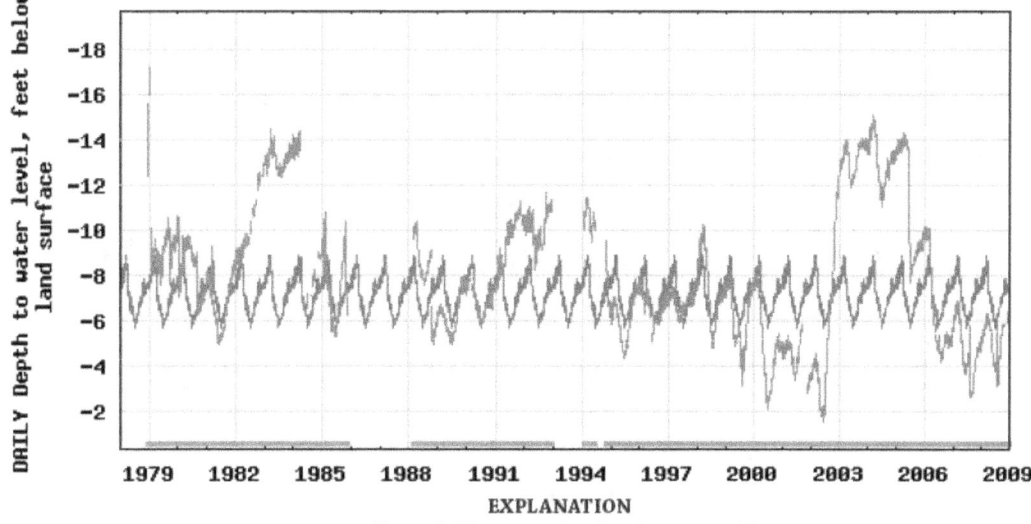

EXPLANATION

—— Median daily statistic (22 years)
—— Daily mean depth to water level
—— Estimated daily mean depth to water level
▬▬ Period of approved data

Figure 25.   Periodic and daily mean water levels in well 33H188, Lower Floridan aquifer, Glynn County Georgia, 1978–2008

Lower Floridan aquifer

310925081312201   Site Name: **33H206**
Glynn County   Period of Record: 1983–2008
Well Depth: 1,100 feet   Datum: 7.00 feet   NGVD 29   Well Diameter: 10.00 inches

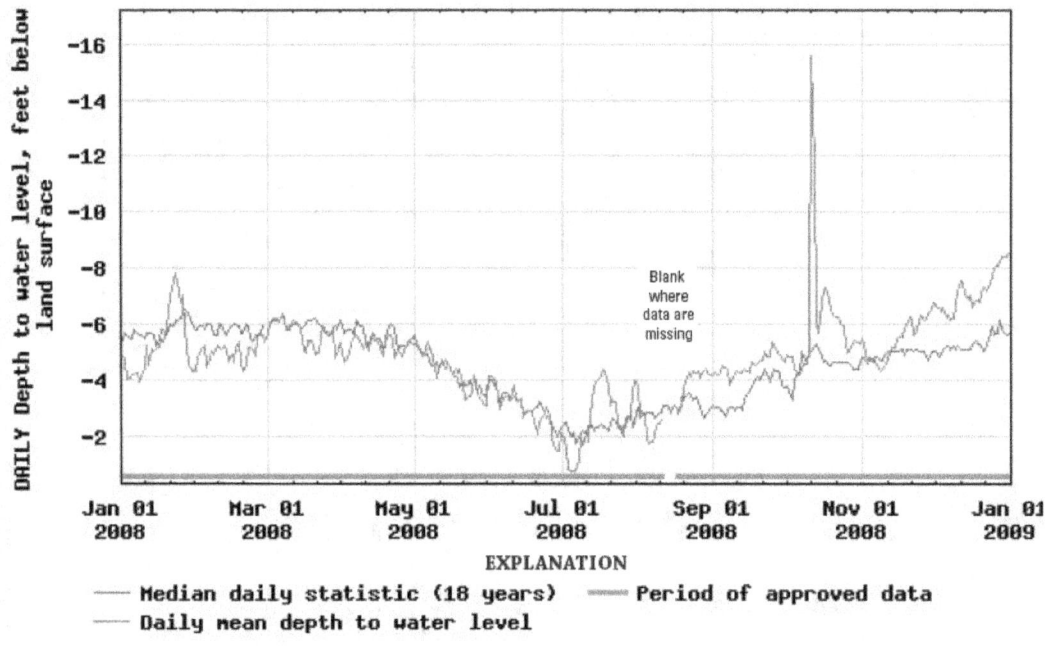

EXPLANATION

—— Median daily statistic (18 years)   ▬▬▬ Period of approved data
—— Daily mean depth to water level

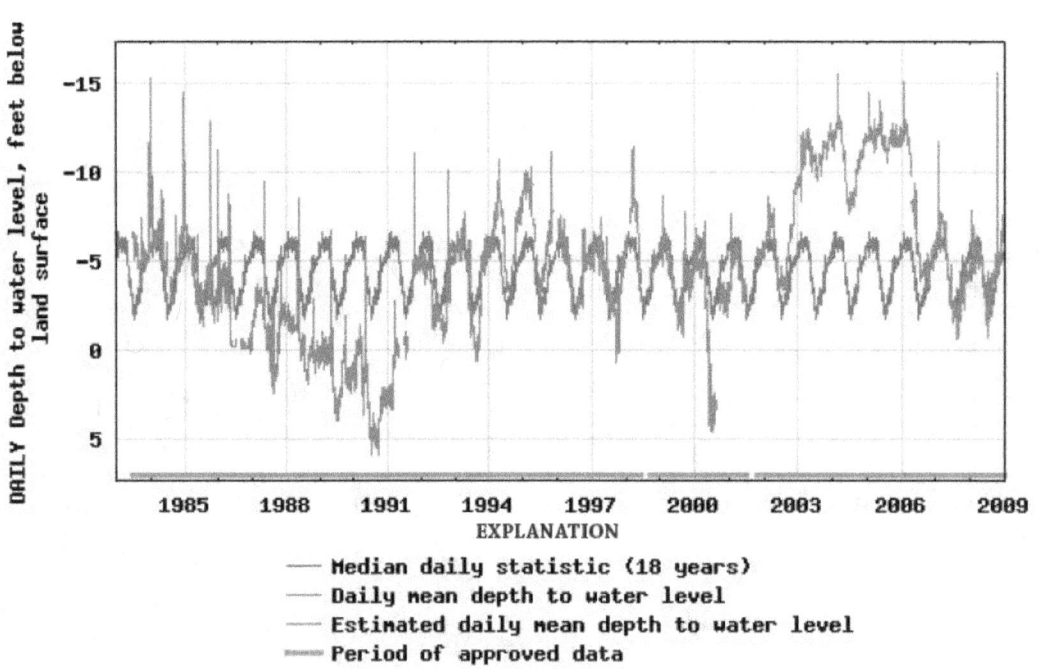

EXPLANATION

—— Median daily statistic (18 years)
—— Daily mean depth to water level
—— Estimated daily mean depth to water level
▬▬▬ Period of approved data

Figure 26.   Periodic and daily mean water levels in well 33H206, Lower Floridan aquifer, Glynn County, Georgia 1983–2008

Lower Floridan aquifer

311633081324001   Site Name: 33J044
Glynn County   Period of Record: 1979–2008
Well Depth: 1,910 feet   Datum: 20.0 feet NGVD 29   Well Diameter: 9.00 inches

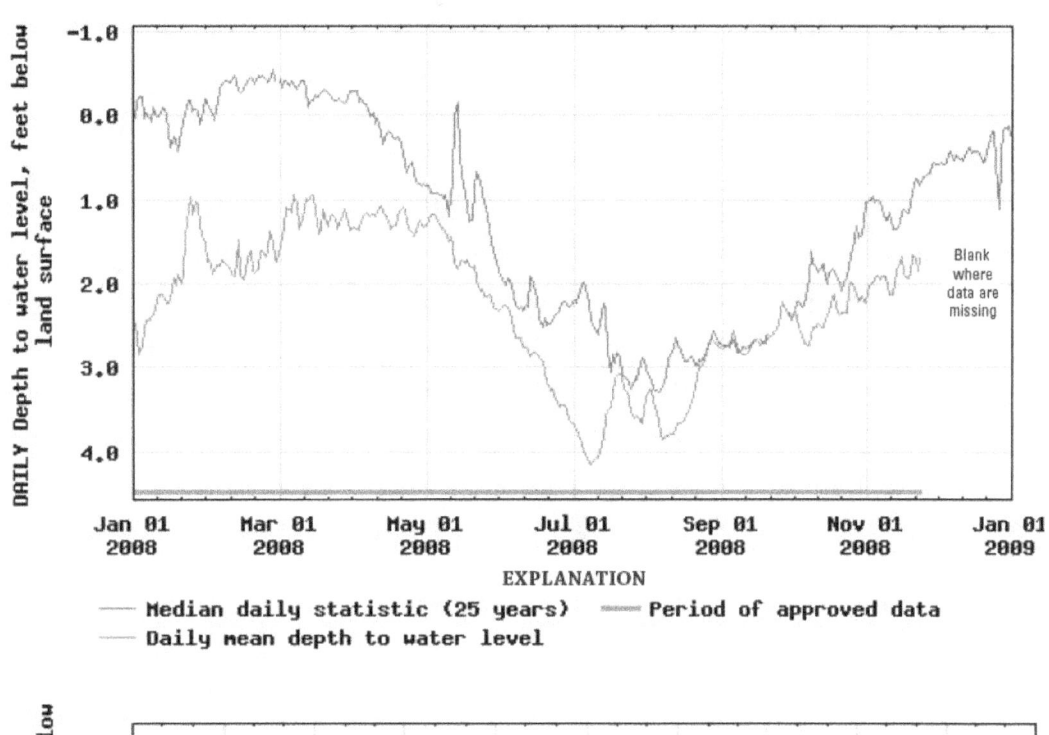

EXPLANATION

—— Median daily statistic (25 years)   ▬▬▬ Period of approved data
—— Daily mean depth to water level

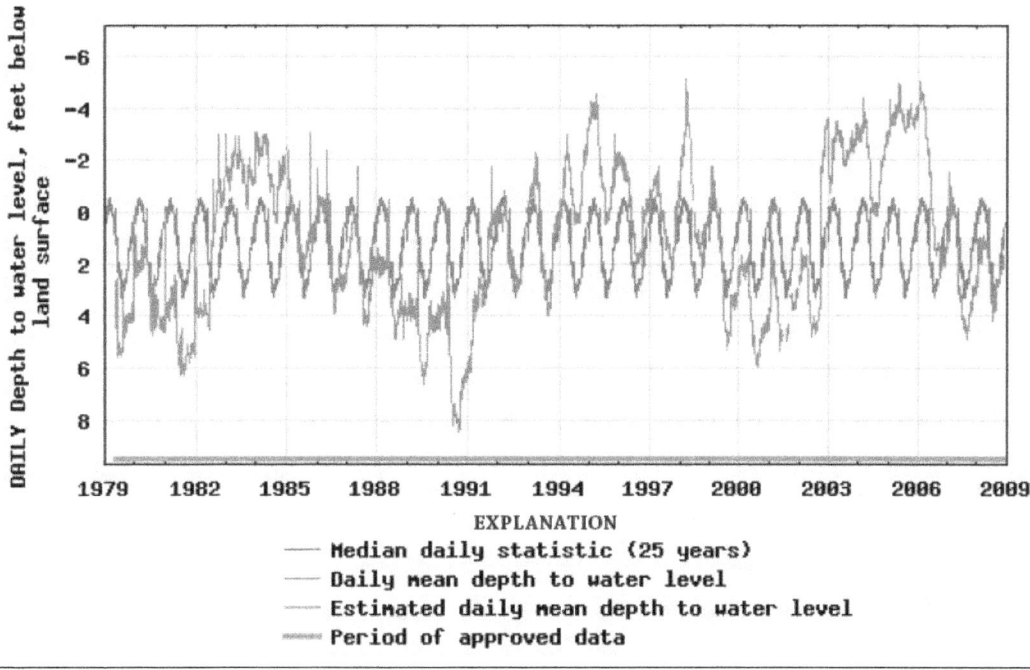

EXPLANATION

—— Median daily statistic (25 years)
—— Daily mean depth to water level
—— Estimated daily mean depth to water level
▬▬▬ Period of approved data

Figure 27.   Periodic and daily mean water levels in well 33J044, Lower Floridan aquifer, Glynn County Georgia 1979–2008.

Lower Floridan aquifer

310818081294201   Site Name: **34H391**
Glynn County   Period of Record: 1975–2008
Well Depth: 1,158 feet   Datum: 7.13 feet   NGVD 29   Well Diameter: 4.00 inches

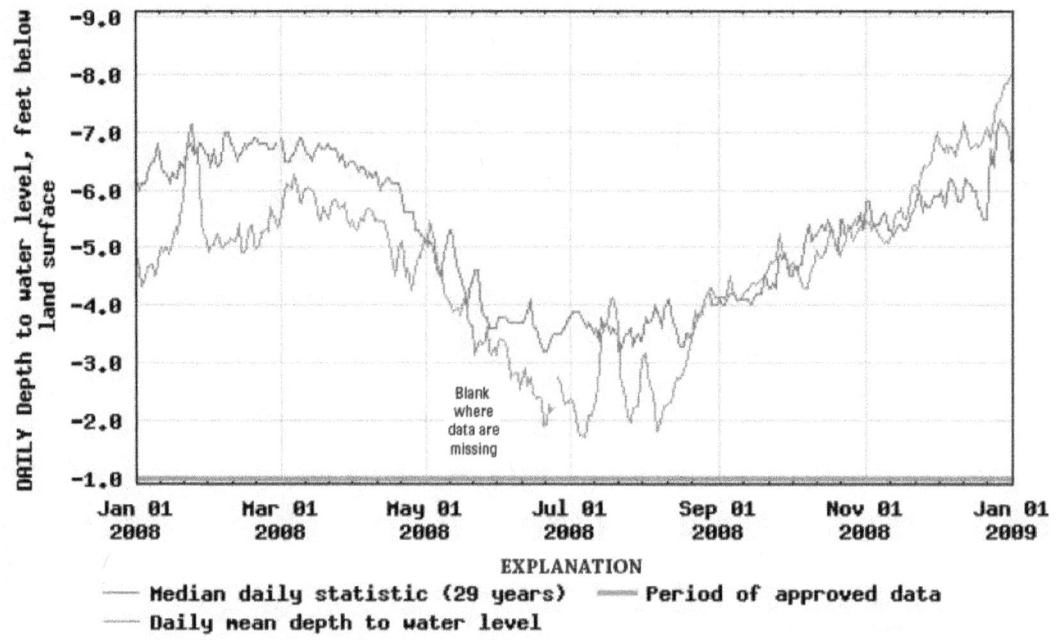

EXPLANATION

— Median daily statistic (29 years)   — Period of approved data
— Daily mean depth to water level

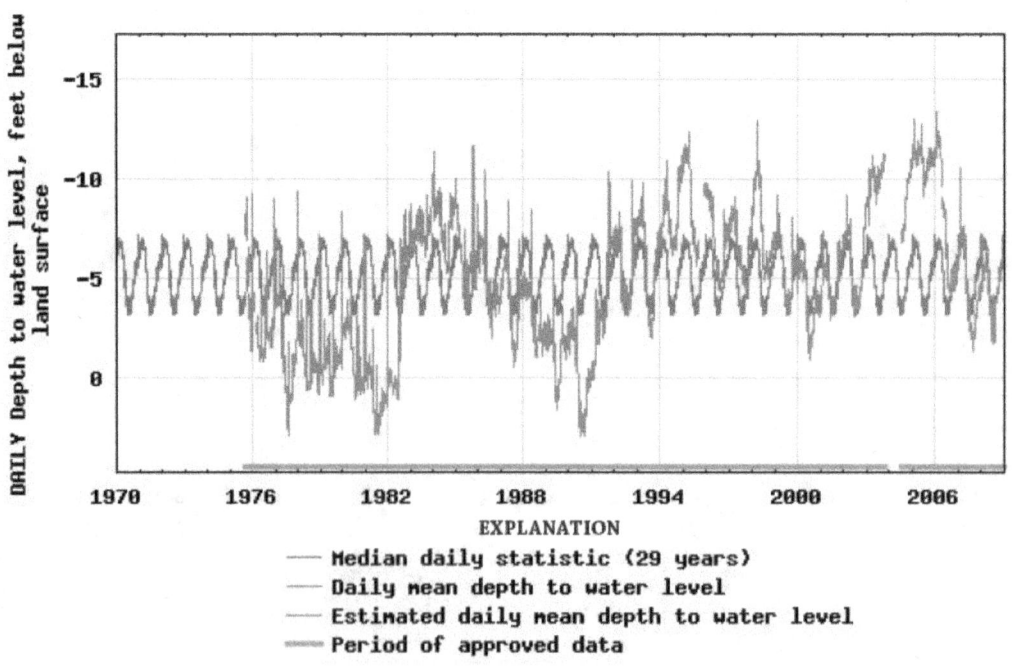

EXPLANATION

— Median daily statistic (29 years)
— Daily mean depth to water level
— Estimated daily mean depth to water level
— Period of approved data

Figure 28.   Periodic and daily mean water levels in well 34H391, Lower Floridan aquifer, Glynn County, Georgia, 1975–2008.

Lower Floridan aquifer

310901081284401   Site Name: 34H436
Glynn County   Period of Record: 1983–2008
Well Depth: 1,103 feet   Datum: 6.62 feet NGVD 29 Well Diameter: 4.00 inches

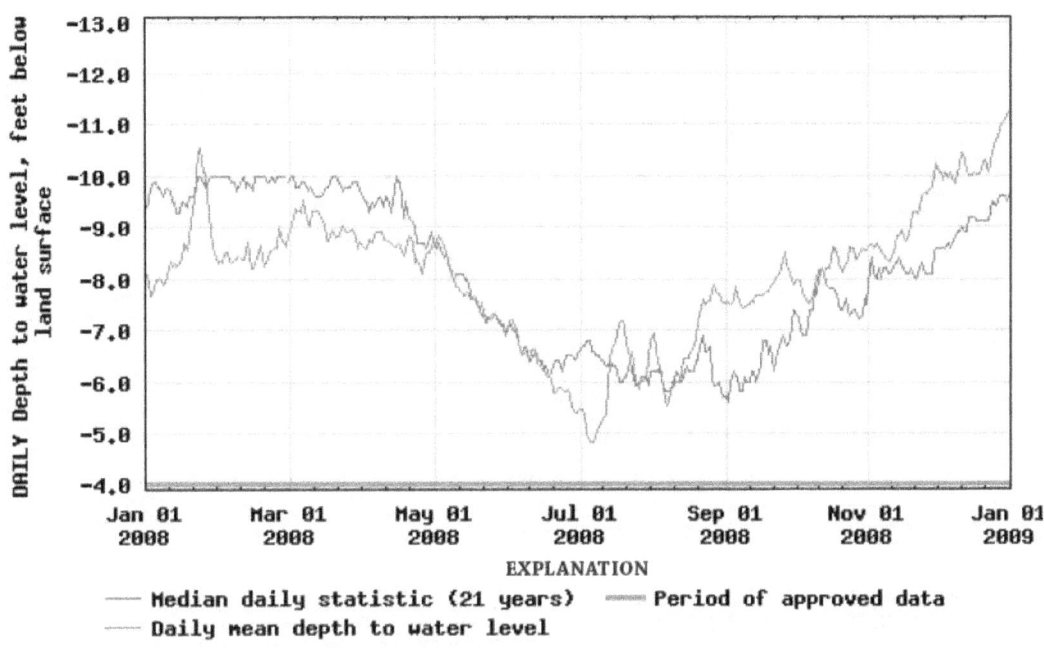

EXPLANATION
—— Median daily statistic (21 years)   ▬▬ Period of approved data
—— Daily mean depth to water level

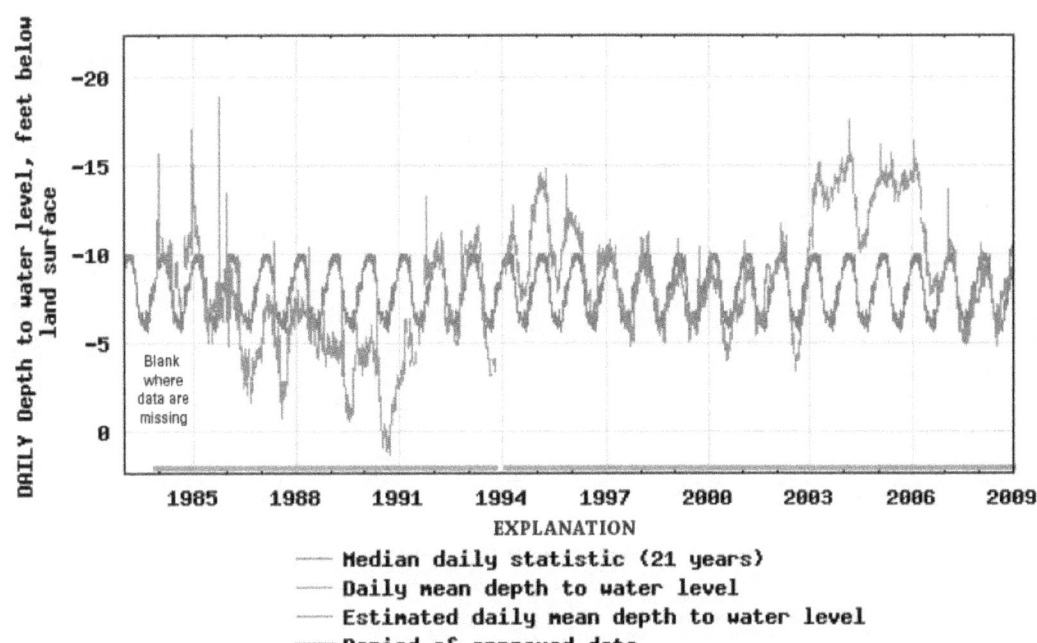

EXPLANATION
——— Median daily statistic (21 years)
——— Daily mean depth to water level
——— Estimated daily mean depth to water level
▬▬▬ Period of approved data

Figure 29.   Periodic and daily mean water levels in well 34H436, Lower Floridan aquifer, Glynn County, Georgia, 1983–2008

Lower Floridan aquifer

310835081294501   Site Name: 34H495

Glynn County   Period of Record: 2001–2008

Well Depth: 2,720 feet   Datum: 10 feet NGVD 29   Well Diameter: 8.00 inches

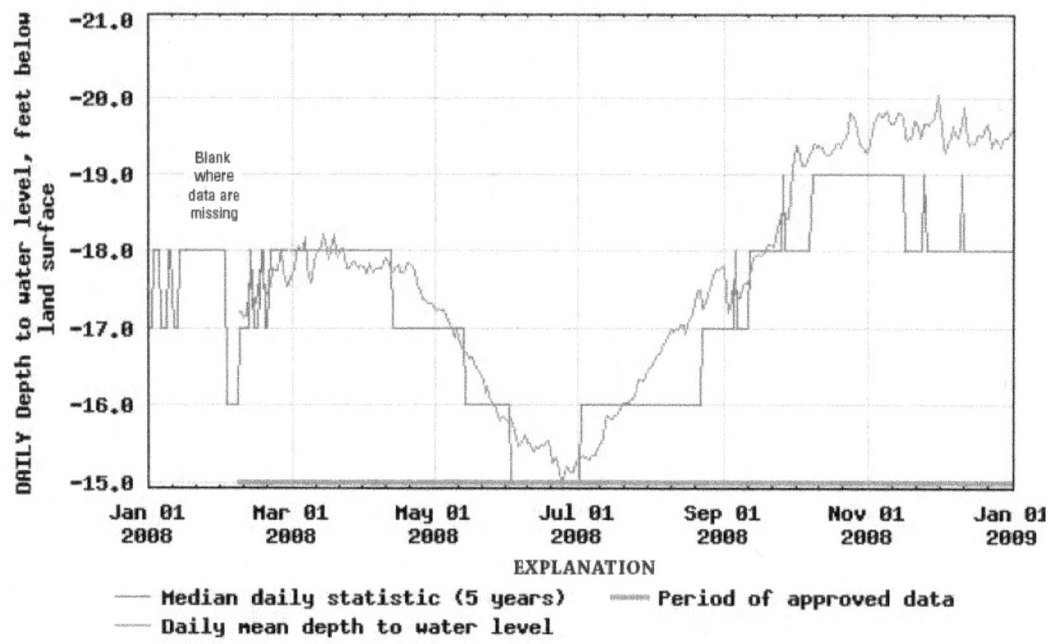

EXPLANATION

—— Median daily statistic (5 years)   ▭▭▭ Period of approved data
—— Daily mean depth to water level

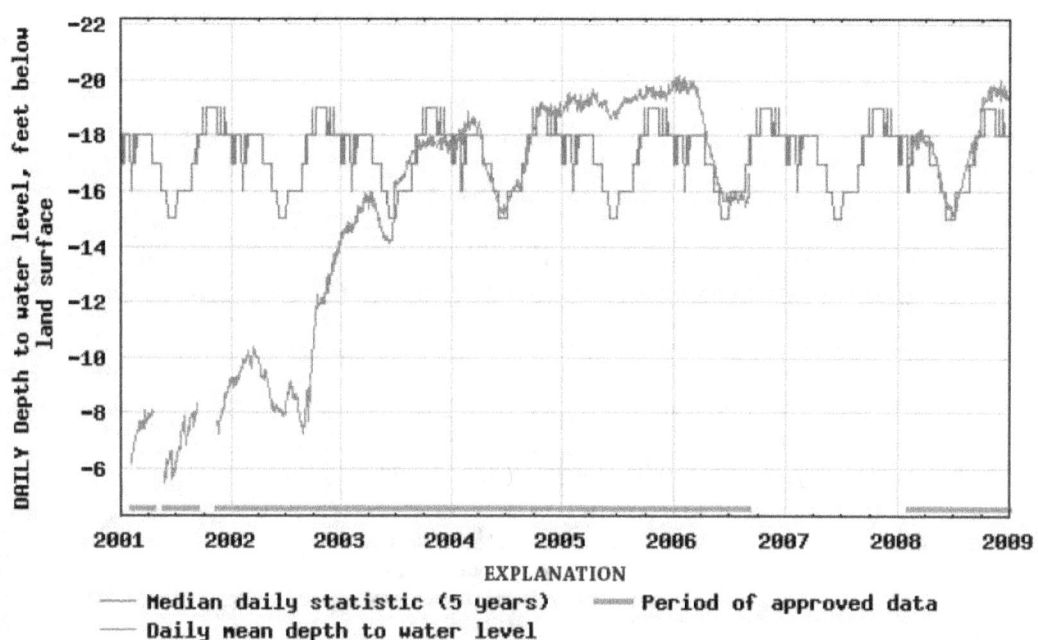

EXPLANATION

—— Median daily statistic (5 years)   ▭▭▭ Period of approved data
—— Daily mean depth to water level

Figure 30.   Periodic and daily mean water levels in well 34H495, Lower Floridan aquifer, Glynn County, Georgia, 2001–2008.

Lower Floridan aquifer

310835081294502   Site Name: 34H500

Glynn County   Period of Record: 2001–2008

Well Depth: 1,400 feet   Datum: 10 feet NGVD 29   Well Diameter: 8.0 inches

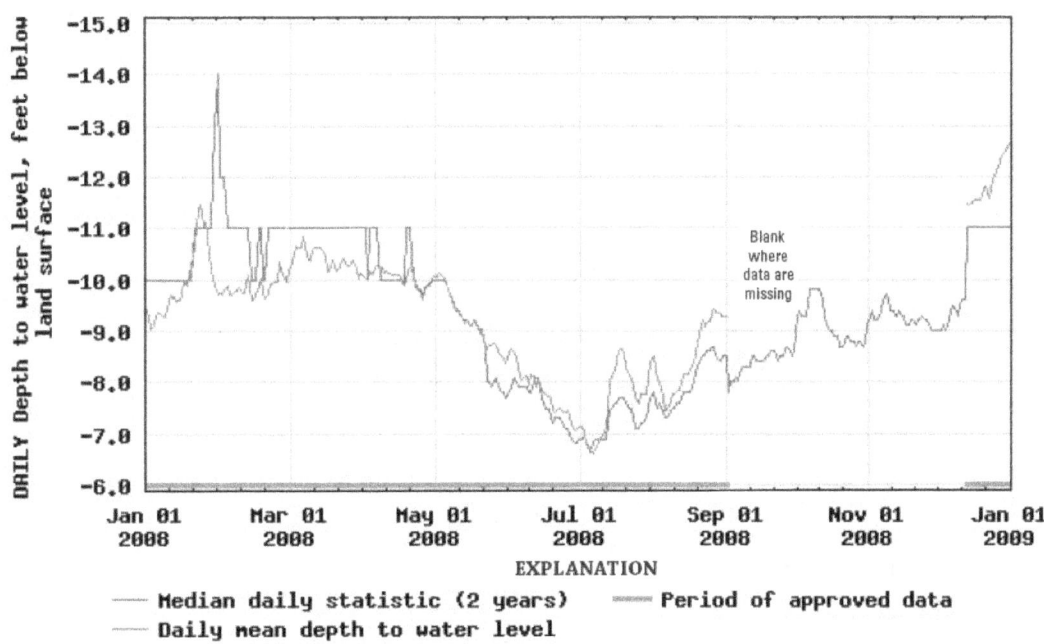

EXPLANATION

—— Median daily statistic (2 years)   ▓▓▓▓ Period of approved data
—— Daily mean depth to water level

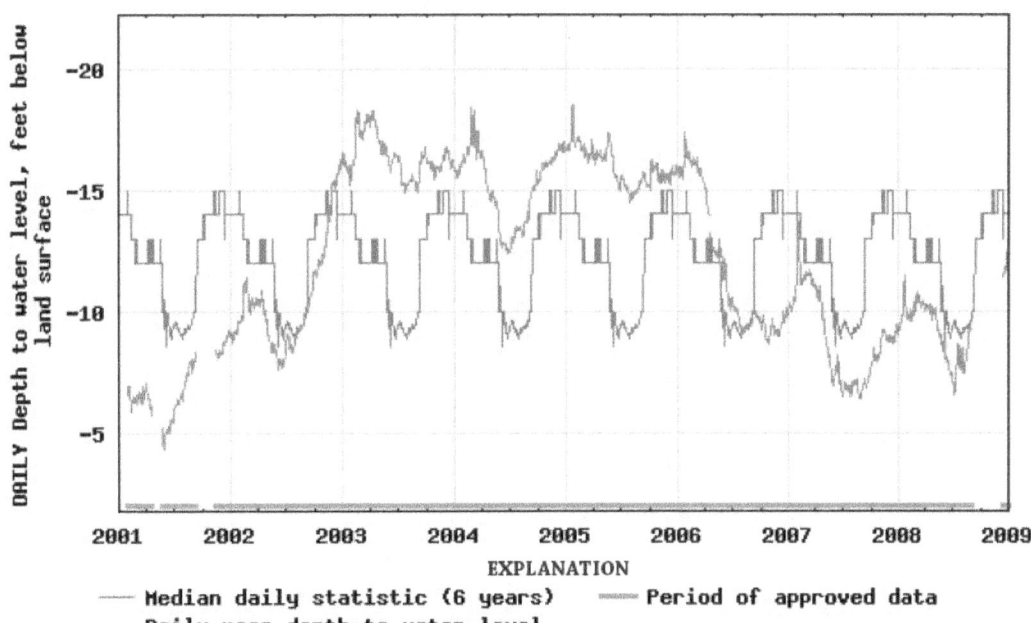

EXPLANATION

—— Median daily statistic (6 years)   ▓▓▓▓ Period of approved data
—— Daily mean depth to water level

Figure 31.   Periodic and daily mean water levels in well 34H500 Lower Floridan aquifer, Glynn County, Georgia, 2001–2008

Chloride Concentrations

Chloride concentrations have been monitored in the Brunswick area since the late 1950s when saltwater was first detected in wells completed in the Upper Floridan aquifer in the southernmost part of Brunswick (Wait, 1965). Saltwater has migrated upward from deep saline zones through

breaches in confining units as a result of reduced pressure in water-bearing zones of the Upper Floridan aquifer. By the 1960s, chloride-contaminated groundwater had migrated northward toward two major industrial pumping centers. Currently (2009), the USGS collects and analyzes samples from a network of wells on an annual basis as part of the CWP (fig. 32; table 2).

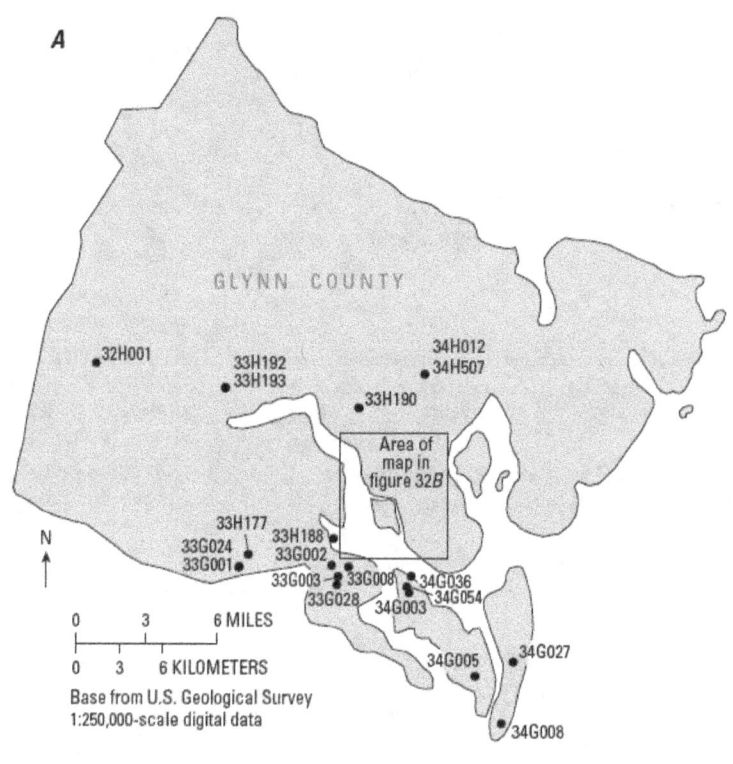

EXPLANATION

●³²ᴴ⁰⁰¹ Well with chloride concentration data and site name

Figure 32. Chloride-monitoring network for the Brunswick–Glynn County area, Georgia: *(A)* location and *(B)* enlarged area.

Explanation

○ 34G002   Well with chloride concentration data and site name

Figure 32   Chloride-monitoring network for the Brunswick–Glynn County area, Georgia:
(A) location and *(B)* enlarged area.—Continued

Table 2. Chloride concentrations and specific conductance in water samples collected from wells in the Brunswick–Glynn County area, Georgia, July and August 2007 (chloride only) and July 2008.

[well locations shown in figs. 34*A* and 34*B*; aquifer or system: S–Surficial, BAS–Brunswick aquifer system, LBA–lower Brunswick aquifer, UFA–Upper Floridan aquifer, FAS–Floridan aquifer system, LFA–Lower Floridan aquifer; μS/cm, microsiemens per centimeter; —, no data]

Well identification	Aquifer or system	Subunit	July and August 2007	July 2008		
			Chloride, in milligrams per liter	Chloride, in milligrams per liter	Change in chloride concentration from 2007	Specific conductance, in μS/cm
34H428	S	None	13.3	13.5	0.2	481
34H515*	S	None	5,250	5,450	200	—
33G028	BAS	None	14.8	—	—	—
33G002	UFA	Upper water-bearing zone	73.4	76.3	2.9	737
33G008	UFA	Upper water-bearing zone	30.0	32.7	2.7	504
33G024	UFA	Upper water-bearing zone	17.7	18.2	0.5	466
34G002	UFA	Upper water-bearing zone	72.1	79.8	7.7	713
34G003	UFA	Upper water-bearing zone	150	—	—	—
34G005	UFA	Upper water-bearing zone	26.4	26.5	0.1	499
34G027	UFA	Upper water-bearing zone	27.6	—	—	—
34G054	UFA	Upper water-bearing zone	44.5	45.3	0.8	580
32H001	BAS	None	27.9	28.5	0.6	466
33H120	UFA	Upper water-bearing zone	22.5	25.4	2.9	489
33H130	UFA	Upper water-bearing zone	2,540	2,480	−60	9,000
33H133	UFA	Upper water-bearing zone	2,180	2,080	−100	7,770
33H177	UFA	Upper water-bearing zone	25.0	24.3	−0.7	549
33H183	UFA	Upper water-bearing zone	—	23.8	—	—
33H190	UFA	Upper water-bearing zone	22.5	22.3	−0.2	462
33H193	UFA	Upper water-bearing zone	18.0	18.6	1	433
33H207	UFA	Upper water-bearing zone	23.2	16.1	−7.1	480
33H211	UFA	Upper water-bearing zone	21.3	18.2	−3.1	459
33H213	UFA	Upper water-bearing zone	49.1	33.7	−15.4	592
33H221	UFA	Upper and lower water-bearing zone	—	372	—	1,960
34H095	UFA	Upper water-bearing zone	30.8	28.9	−1.9	502
34H112	UFA	Upper water-bearing zone	1,450	1,430	−20	5,300
34H117	UFA	Upper water-bearing zone	551	545	−6.0	2,380
34H125	UFA	Upper water-bearing zone	360	321	−39	1,660
34H334	UFA	Lower water-bearing zone	1,090	1,070	−20.0	4,240
34H344	UFA	Upper water-bearing zone	30.0	26.2	−3.8	480
34H355	UFA	Upper water-bearing zone	326	341	15	1,620
34H363	UFA	Upper water-bearing zone	80.9	—	—	—
34H371*	UFA	Upper water-bearing zone	15.2	15.4	0.2	451
34H373	UFA	Upper water-bearing zone	353	349	−4.0	1,770
34H374	UFA	Upper water-bearing zone	981	995	14	4,110
34H392	UFA	Upper water-bearing zone	18.7	19.2	0.5	422
34H393	UFA	Upper water-bearing zone	1,870	1,880	10	6,820
34H400	UFA	Upper water-bearing zone	433	422	−11	1,970

Table 2. Chloride concentrations and specific conductance in water samples collected from wells in the Brunswick–Glynn County area, Georgia, July and August 2007 (chloride only) and July 2008.—Continued

[well locations shown in figs. 34A and 34B; aquifer or system: S–Surficial, BAS–Brunswick aquifer system, LBA–lower Brunswick aquifer, UFA–Upper Floridan aquifer, FAS–Floridan aquifer system, LFA–Lower Floridan aquifer; µS/cm, microsiemens per centimeter; —, no data]

Well identification	Aquifer or system	Subunit	July and August 2007	July 2008		
			Chloride, in milligrams per liter	Chloride, in milligrams per liter	Change in chloride concentration from 2007	Specific conductance, in µS/cm
34H401	UFA	Upper water-bearing zone	1,800	1,890	90	7,170
34H413	UFA	Upper water-bearing zone	—	416	—	1,980
34H424	UFA	Upper water-bearing zone	2,180	2,220	40	7,990
34H425	UFA	Upper water-bearing zone	269	241	−28	1,310
34H427	UFA	Upper water-bearing zone	1,390	1,360	−30	5,280
34H434	UFA	Upper water-bearing zone	1,620	1,460	−160	5,510
34H445	UFA	Upper water-bearing zone	18.4	18.9	0.5	450
34H449	UFA	Upper water-bearing zone	27.5	27.8	0.3	498
34H450	UFA	Upper water-bearing zone	16.6	16.9	0.3	454
34H469	UFA	Upper water-bearing zone	894	878	−16	3,540
34H552	UFA	Upper water-bearing zone	31.3	—	—	—
33G003	FAS	Upper and lower water-bearing zone	39.5	—	—	—
33H127	FAS	Lower water-bearing zone	863	902	39	3,620
33H154	FAS	Lower water-bearing zone	2,210	2,200	−10	8,110
33H189	FAS	Upper and lower water-bearing zone	—	—	—	—
33H212	FAS	Lower water-bearing zone	1,100	1,170	70	4,860
33H214	FAS	Lower water-bearing zone	124	—	—	—
34H076	FAS	Upper and lower water-bearing zone	974	936	−38	3,740
34H134	FAS	Upper and lower water-bearing zone	34.8	57.6	23	593
34H354	FAS	Lower water-bearing zone	1,440	1,460	20	5,680
34H398	FAS	Upper water-bearing zone	137	137	0	1,030
34H402	FAS	Lower water-bearing zone	2,350	2,340	−10	8,900
34H403	FAS	Upper and lower water-bearing zone	1,380	1,380	0	5,160
33G001	UFA, LFA	None	34.0	35.1	1.1	601
34G036	LFA	None	479	477	−2.0	2,190
33H188	LFA	Fernandina permeable zone	9,910	9,750	−160	32,900
33H192	LFA	None	744	700	−44	8,160
33H206	LFA	None	389	567	178	2,070
34H391	LFA	None	2,740	2,640	−100	9,240
34H399	LFA	None	6,940	7,530	590	21,700
34H426	LFA	None	542	482	−60	2,280
34H436	LFA	None	20.8	20.7	−0.1	518

*Replaced well 34H438

Upper Floridan Aquifer

The area of chloride contamination in the Upper Floridan aquifer at Brunswick during July 2008 was mapped based on samples from 26 wells (fig. 33). During this period, the chloride concentration was greater than 250 mg/L, the State and Federal secondary drinking-water standard (Georgia Environmental Protection Division, 1997; U.S. Environmental Protection Agency, 2000), in an approximate 2-mi^2 area and exceeded 2,250 mg/L in part of the area. Yearly fluctuations of chloride concentration indicate increases as much as 90 mg/L and decreases as much as 100 mg/L from 2007 to 2008 (fig. 34; table 2). The July 2008 map (fig. 33) is similar to previously published maps for 2007 (Cherry and Clarke, 2008) and shows that areas of highest concentration are near the two industrial pumping centers in the northern part of the city of Brunswick, as well as the original area of contamination in the southern part of the city.

Graphs of chloride concentrations in water samples from wells with open intervals in the upper and lower water-bearing zones of the Upper Floridan aquifer are shown for the southern Brunswick area (34H393 and 34H403, fig. 35) and northern Brunswick area (33H133 and 33H127, fig. 36). Chloride concentration in water from the Lower Floridan aquifer is shown for well 34H391 in the southern Brunswick area (fig. 35). Additional information about water-quality monitoring in the Brunswick area can be accessed at *http://ga.water.usgs.gov/projects/brunswick/*.

During July 2008, chloride concentrations in the Brunswick area generally were lower than in 2007, with decreases as much as 100 mg/L in the northwestern part of the area (fig. 34). Chloride concentrations in the southern Brunswick area continued to decrease in well 34H393 and 34H391 and remained about the same in well 34H403 since 2007 (fig. 35). In the northern Brunswick area, chloride concentrations have increased since the 1960s, reflecting influences of local pumping (fig. 36). During 2007–2008, chloride concentrations decreased in well 33H133 and increased slightly in well 33H127 (fig. 36; table 2).

Outside the plume area, chloride concentrations are less than the 250 mg/L drinking-water standard (fig. 33; table 2). However, local areas have chloride concentrations greater than 50 mg/L, which is considered to be greater than background levels, and includes concentrations in wells 34G002 and 34H398 (fig. 32; table 2). The reason for elevated chloride concentrations in these wells remains unclear, but elevated concentrations could be related to failed or improper well-casing seals (Hall and Peck, 2005).

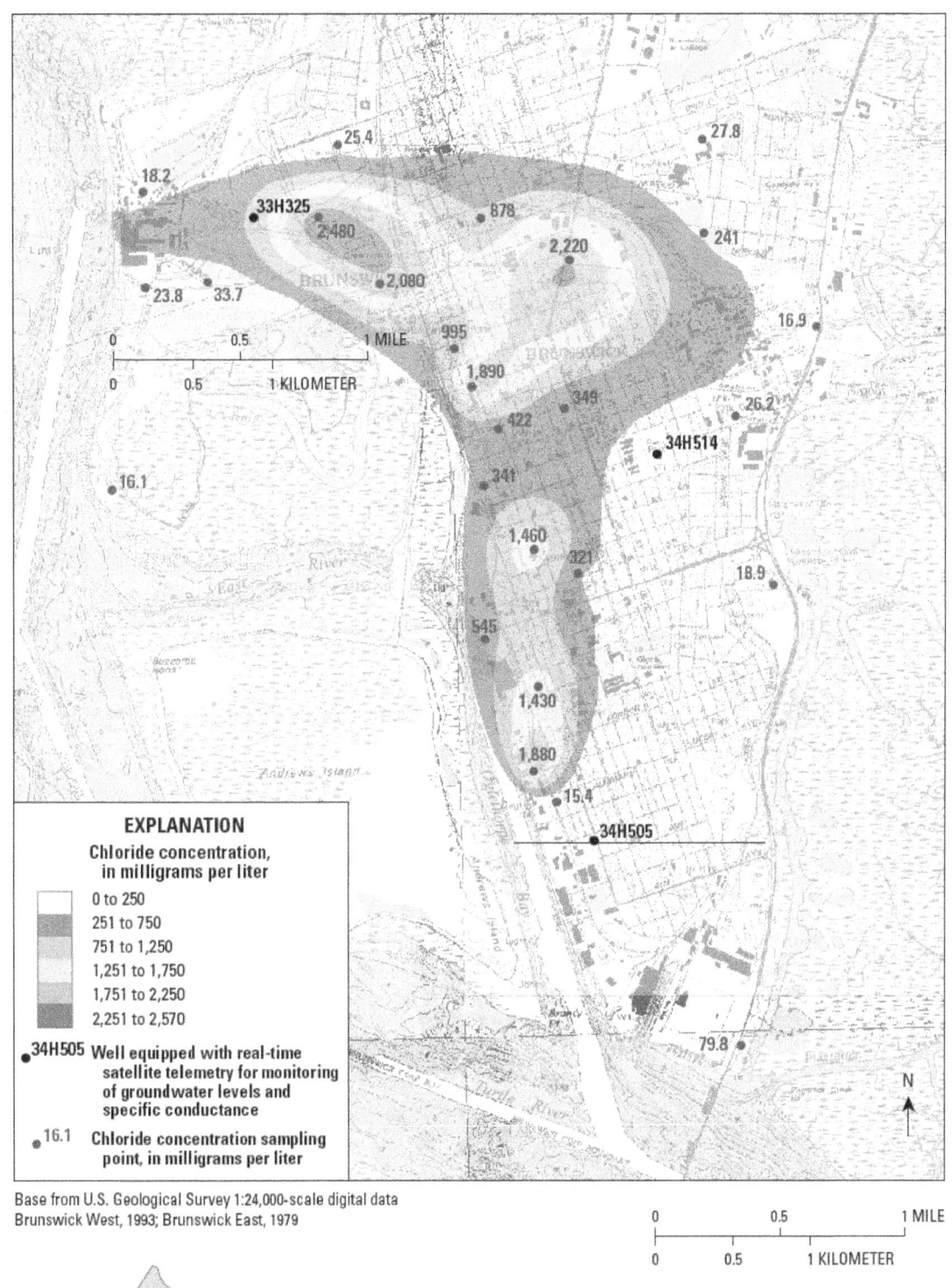

EXPLANATION

Chloride concentration, in milligrams per liter

	0 to 250
	251 to 750
	751 to 1,250
	1,251 to 1,750
	1,751 to 2,250
	2,251 to 2,570

●34H505   Well equipped with real-time satellite telemetry for monitoring of groundwater levels and specific conductance

●16.1   Chloride concentration sampling point, in milligrams per liter

Base from U.S. Geological Survey 1:24,000-scale digital data
Brunswick West, 1993; Brunswick East, 1979

Glynn County

Area of enlarged map

Figure 33.   Chloride concentration in the Upper Floridan aquifer in the Brunswick–Glynn County area, Georgia, July 2008.

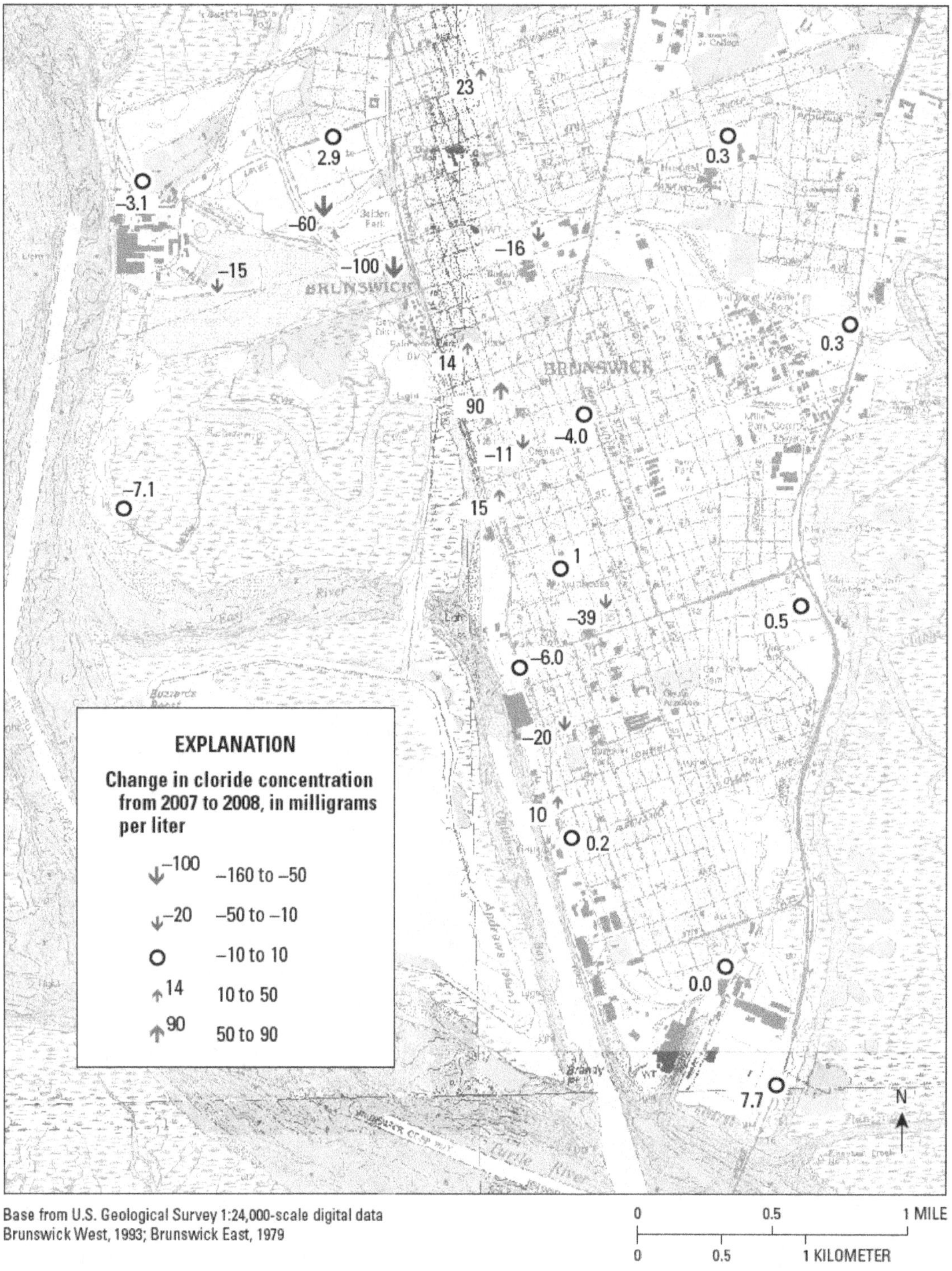

EXPLANATION

Change in cloride concentration from 2007 to 2008, in milligrams per liter

$\downarrow^{-100}$	−160 to −50
$\downarrow^{-20}$	−50 to −10
$\circ$	−10 to 10
$\uparrow^{14}$	10 to 50
$\uparrow^{90}$	50 to 90

Base from U.S. Geological Survey 1:24,000-scale digital data
Brunswick West, 1993; Brunswick East, 1979

0   0.5   1 MILE

0   0.5   1 KILOMETER

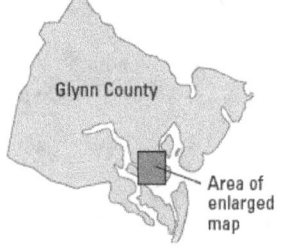

Glynn County

Area of enlarged map

Figure 34. Change in chloride concentration in the Upper Floridan aquifer in the Brunswick–Glynn County area, Georgia, from 2007 to 2008.

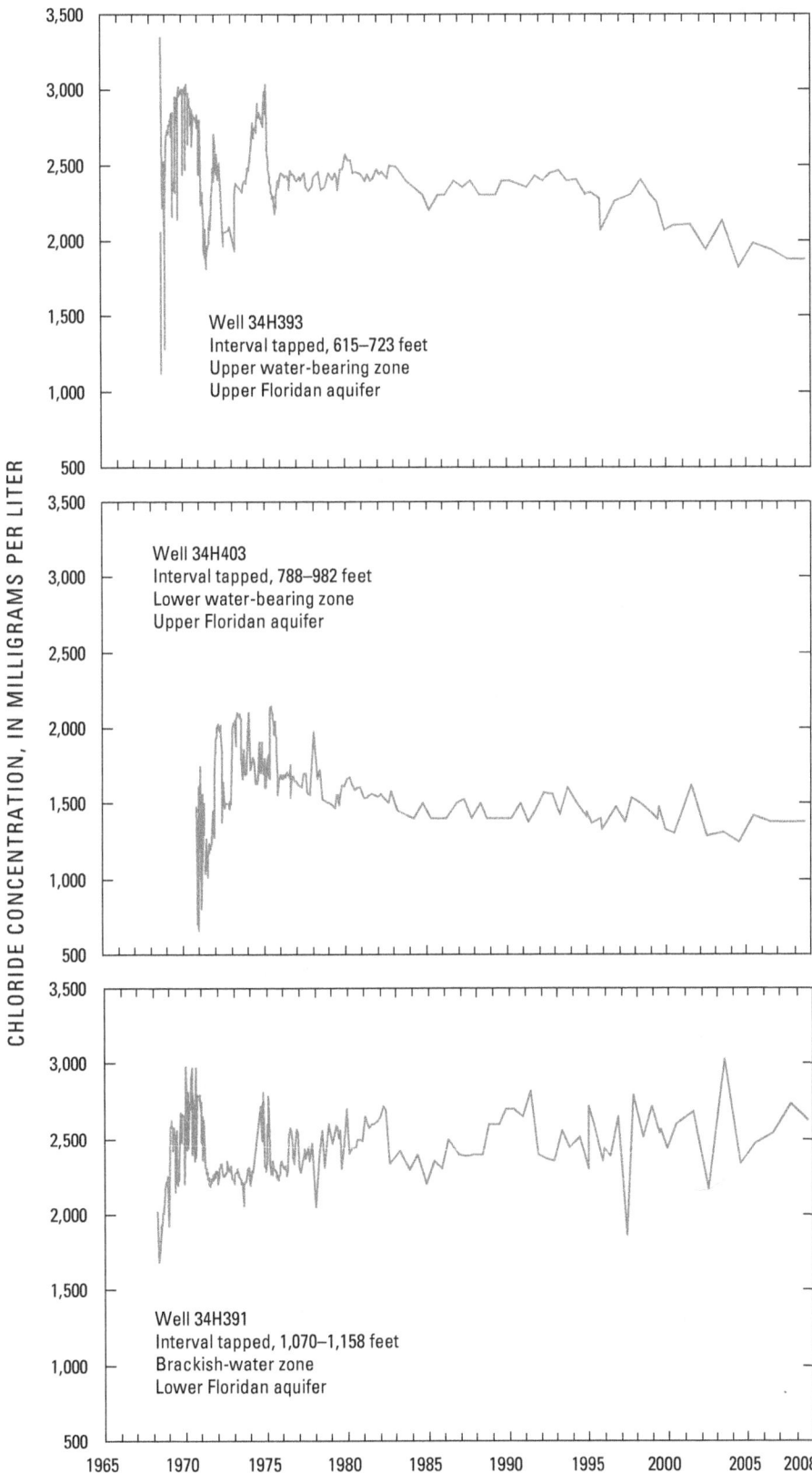

Figure 35.   Chlor de concentration in water for selected wells in the southern Brunswick–Glynn County area, Georgia, 1968–2008 (see figure 32*B* for well location).

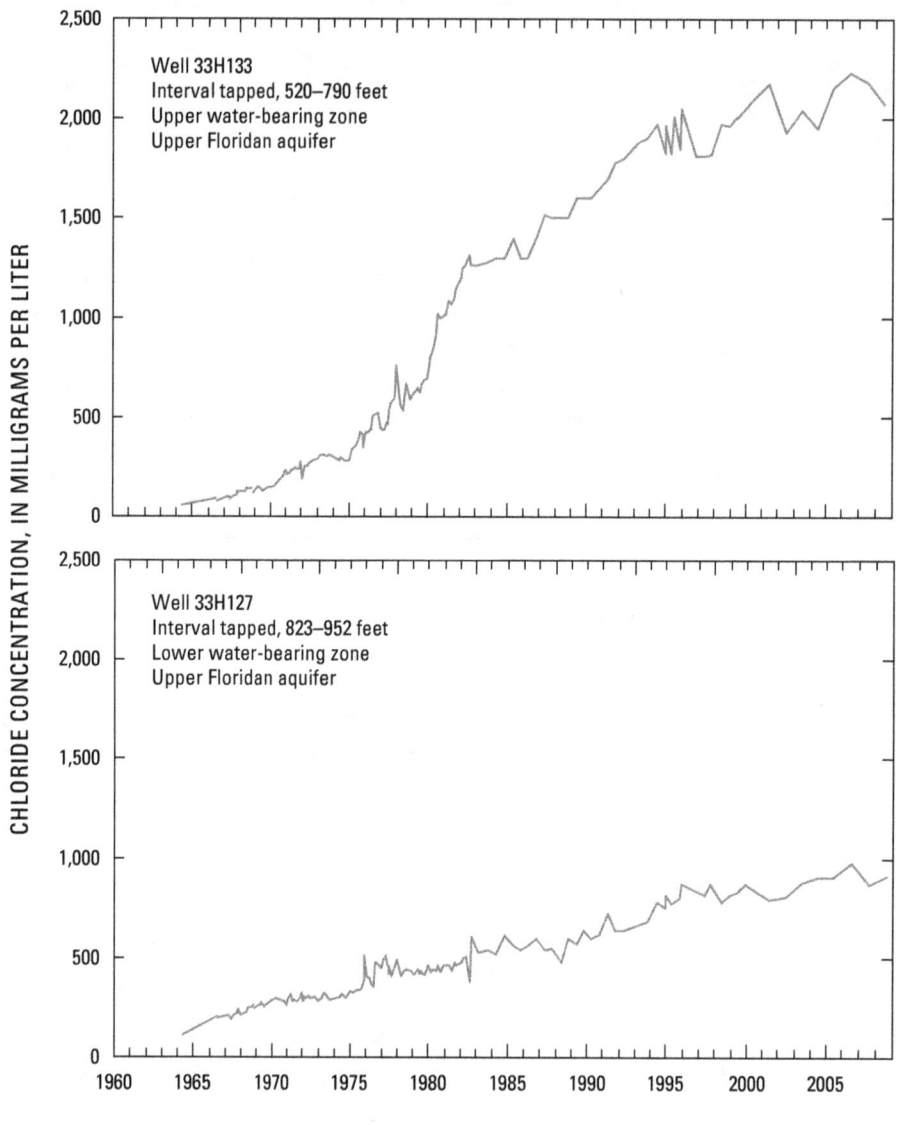

Fig . Chloride concentration in wate for sele ted wells in the northern
Bru I C un , eo 68 2 8 (se fi ure 32 fo w lo tio .

Real-Time Monitoring of Specific Conductance and Water Levels

To monitor the extent of chloride contamination in the Brunswick area, a network of real-time monitoring wells completed in the upper and lower water-bearing zones of the Upper Floridan aquifer was established around the plume (figs. 17, 33). This network includes the Perry Park site (well 34H514) funded by the CWP and the Southside Baptist Church (wells 34H504 and 34H505) and Georgia–Pacific Cellulose (wells 33H324 and 33H325) sites funded by GaEPD (fig. 17). During 2007, each of the five sites was equipped with real-time water-level recorders, and the Perry Park site (well 34H514) was also equipped with a real-time specific conductance monitor. The Southside Baptist Church site (well 34H505) and Georgia–Pacific Cellulose site (33H325) were instrumented for real-time specific conductance monitoring during 2008 (fig. 33). Measurement depths in each well were determined using borehole resistivity and temperature logs to delineate water-bearing zones vulnerable to saltwater contamination (Walls and others, 2009). This equipment measures specific conductance, a surrogate for chloride concentration, to monitor the potential movement of saltwater into groundwater of the Upper Floridan aquifer.

The Perry Park well (34H514), which is immediately outside the plume area, had chloride concentrations that fluctuated in response to pumping changes (fig. 37). The specific conductance at this site during 2007–2008 fluctuated from 423 to 930 microsiemens per centimeter (µS/cm). A correlation between chloride concentration and specific conductance indicates this range in values corresponds to chloride levels that are generally less than 100 mg/L (fig. 38; table 2).

Water levels in the Georgia–Pacific Cellulose wells (33H324 and 33H325) indicate the gradient is downward from the upper into the lower water-bearing zone, the reverse of the naturally occurring gradient between these zones (fig. 39). The water levels in these wells are influenced by pumping because of their close proximity to the production wells at Georgia–Pacific Cellulose, which tap into the upper and the lower water-bearing zones of the Upper Floridan aquifer. Specific conductance at well 33H325 during 2008 fluctuated from 7,090 to 7,420 µS/cm. Using the correlation chart between chloride concentration and specific conductance yields chloride concentrations ranging between 1,900 and 2,000 mg/L (fig. 38).

The Southside Baptist Church wells (34H504 and 34H505) are located outside the plume area and are not influenced by any local pumping in the area. The water levels in these wells indicate that the natural gradient is upward from the lower to the upper water-bearing zone of the Upper Floridan aquifer (fig. 40). The specific conductance at this site during 2008 increased from 973 to 1,940 µS/cm, with a steady rise throughout the entire year. The increasing levels of specific conductance correspond to a period in which the head differentials between the upper and the lower water-bearing zones of the Upper Floridan aquifer are minimized and the gradient is decreased. Using the correlation chart between chloride concentration and specific conductance yields chloride levels ranging between 200 and 500 mg/L (fig. 38). The real-time data are available on the USGS Web site and can be accessed at *http://waterdata.usgs.gov/ga/nwis/current/?type=gw*.

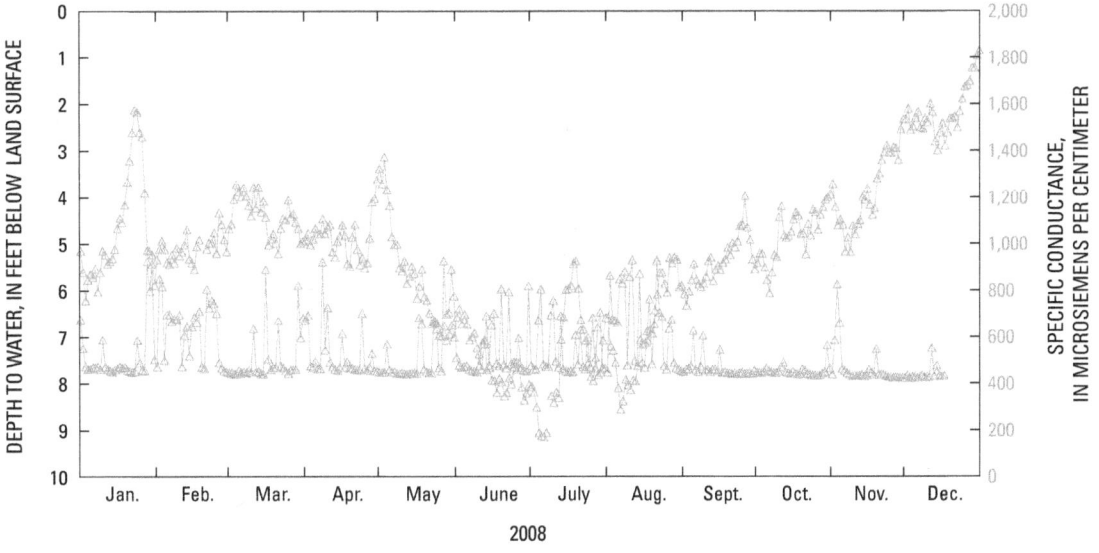

Figure 37. Daily mean groundwater levels and periodic specific conductance in the Upper Floridan aquifer at well 34H514, Perry Park, Brunswick–Glynn County area, Georgia, 2008.

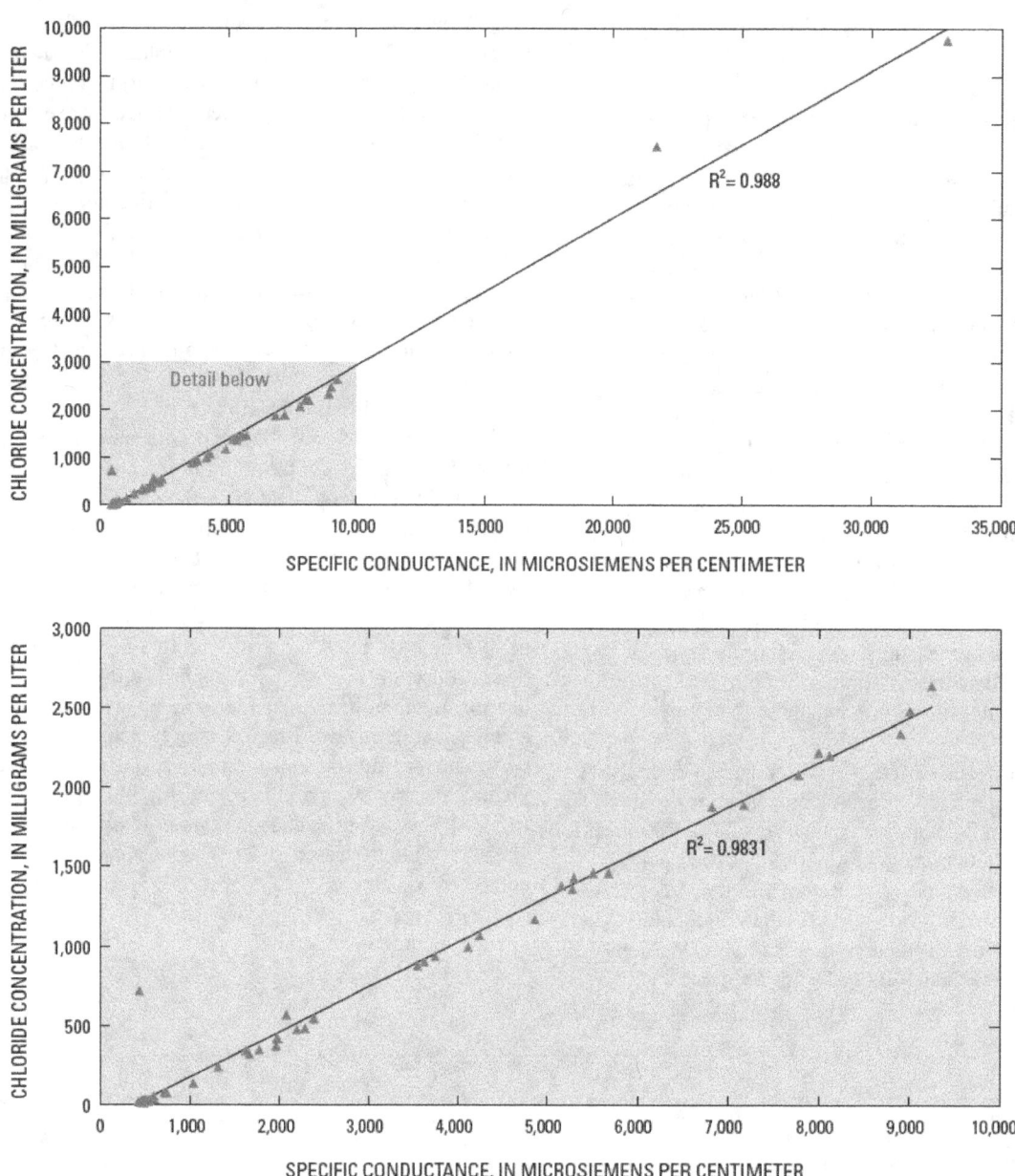

Figure 38.   Correlation betw en chloride concentration and specific conductance from groundwater samples taken in the Brunswick–Glynn County area, Georgia, July 2008.

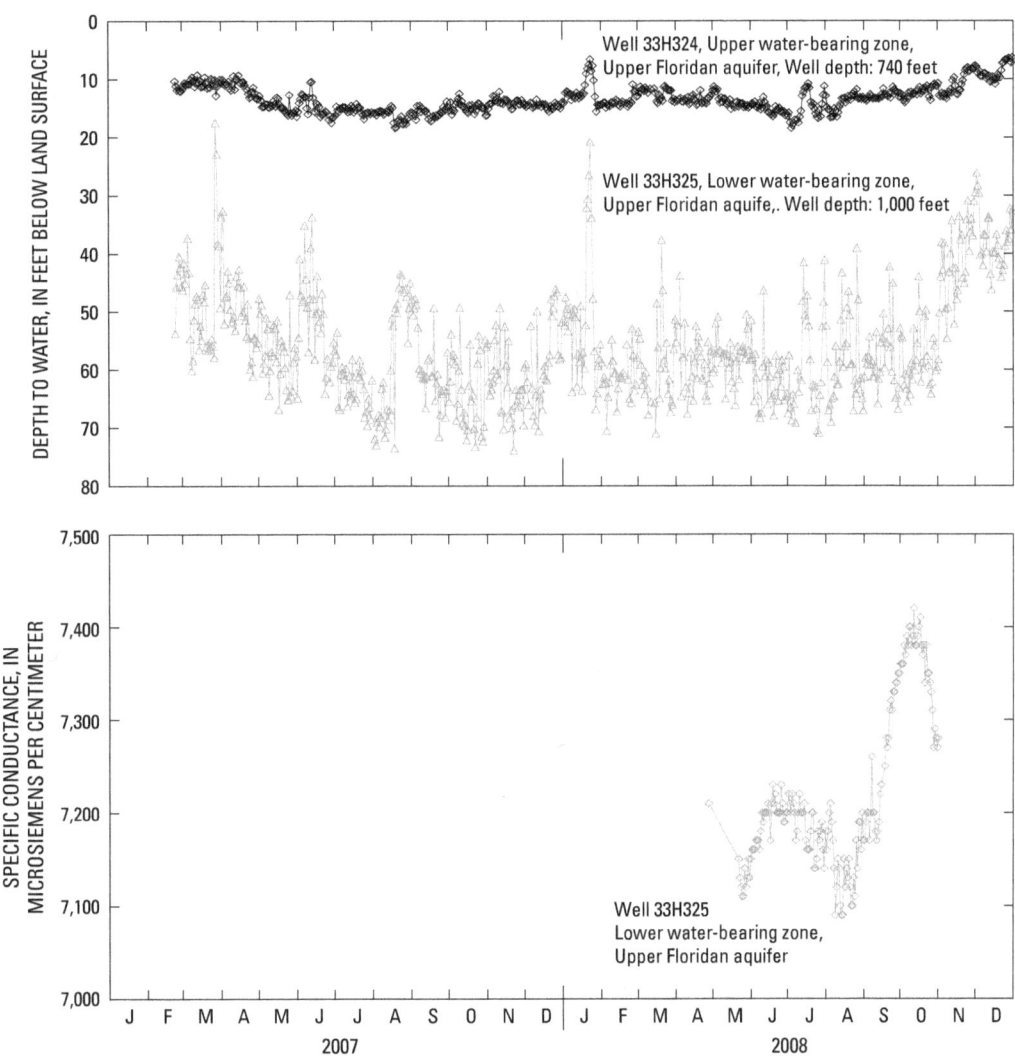

Figure 39.   Daily mean water levels in wells 33H324 and 33H325, and specific conductance in well 33H325 Upper Floridan aquifer, Brunswick–Glynn County area, Georgia, 2008.

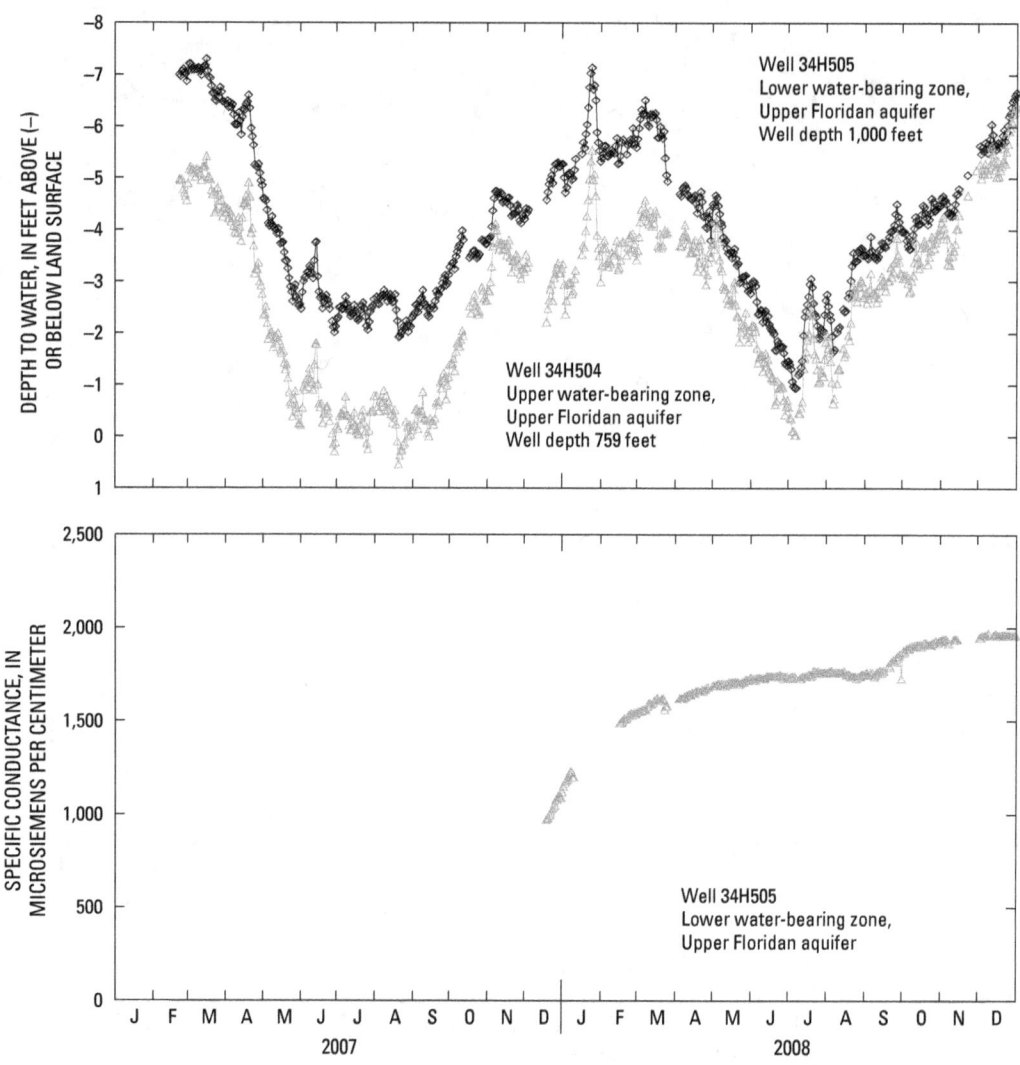

e   Daily mean groundwater levels and peri dic spec fic conductance in the U per
q   r t   w c –   t a

Surficial and Brunswick Aquifer Systems

Historically, water-quality data-collection efforts in the Glynn County area have focused on the Floridan aquifer system. Clarke and others (1990), however, recognized that locally, water-quality problems exist in the surficial and Brunswick aquifer systems. These problems typically can be associated with (1) saltwater encroachment in shallow wells near the coast, tidal rivers, and estuaries; (2) upward leakage of water from underlying aquifers through semiconfining units or fractures as a result of natural or pumping-induced head gradients; or (3) failed well casings. Localized saltwater contamination has been recognized in a number of areas along the coast, including Vernonburg, GA, in Chatham County (Hall and Peck, 2005) and Sea Island, GA, in Glynn County (Julie Vann, Georgia Environmental Protection Division, written commun., July 2005).

During 2008, water samples were collected and analyzed for chloride concentration from two wells completed in the surficial aquifer—well 34H515 and well 34H428 (table 2). Well 34H515 was drilled in 2005 as a replacement well for well 34H438, which had shown a large increase in chloride concentration (fig. 41). The new well produced similar chloride concentrations, verifying the increase indicated by the previous well. The reason for the increase is unknown—no known supply wells are completed in the surficial aquifer in the area nor have there been any changes in land-use practices in the immediate area. The monitoring of chloride concentrations in this well is ongoing. The well is located in close proximity to a saltwater marsh and tidally influenced canals designed to prevent flooding during high tide. The only other well open to the surficial aquifer system (well 34H428) continues to show chloride levels below 20 mg/L.

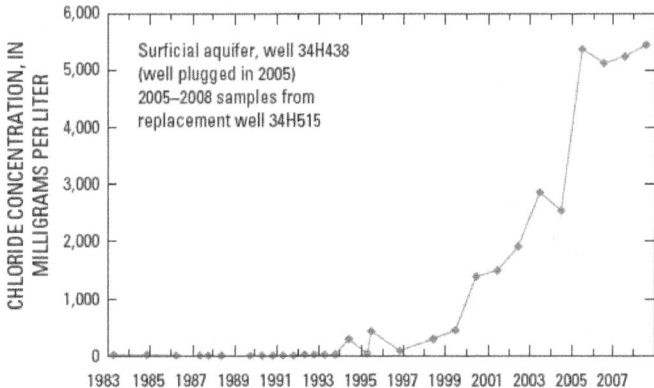

Figure 41. Chloride concentration in well 34H438 and replacement well 34H515, surficial aquifer system, in the Brunswick–Glynn County area, Georgia, 1983–2008 (see figure 32B for well location).

Groundwater Studies

The CWP provides for the ongoing collection of hydrologic data to support a better understanding of the occurrence and controls on saltwater contamination for the evaluation of alternative water sources. In past years, the program has included collecting borehole geophysical logs to characterize physical and chemical properties of hydrogeologic units and conducting field inventories of existing wells to obtain groundwater-level and water-quality data and improve data coverage in the area.

During 2008, the principal focus of groundwater studies for the CWP was the refinement of an existing groundwater-flow model to enable better-detailed simulations in the vicinity of the chloride plume. The model has been designed to evaluate changes in hydraulic gradients near the chloride plume resulting from changes in pumpage (Cherry and Payne, 2007). Currently (2009), the lateral extent of chloride contamination is contained because large groundwater withdrawals create a depression in the potentiometric surface of the Upper Floridan aquifer, and groundwater flows inward from surrounding areas along a hydraulic gradient. If this gradient were reversed because of large-scale pumping outside of the plume area, chloride contaminated groundwater could flow outward in the opposite direction and contaminate fresh-water areas.

The model used in this study, described in detail in Payne and others (2005), uses MODFLOW-2000 (Harbaugh and others, 2000), which is a finite-difference, constant-density flow simulator. The model boundaries extend throughout the coastal Georgia area and into adjacent parts of Florida and South Carolina and encompass an area approximately 42,155 mi^2 (fig. 42). The original MODFLOW model was horizontally discretized using a variably spaced grid with cell sizes ranging from approximately 4,000 x 5,000 ft at Savannah and Brunswick to 16,500 x 16,500 ft near the lateral boundaries (Payne and others, 2005). Grid density is higher at Savannah and Brunswick, Georgia, to enable simulation of steeper head gradients near areas of concentrated pumping. Each unit is represented with one layer of grid cells in the vertical dimension. To enable an even more refined simulation of hydraulic gradients near the Brunswick chloride plume, the grid size for the refined model is reduced to 500 x 500 ft.

The original model (Payne and others, 2005) is comprised of seven aquifers and confining units. These include, in descending order:

- the confined upper and lower water-bearing zones of the surficial aquifer system, grouped together (unit 1);

- the Brunswick aquifer system confining unit (unit 2);

- the upper and lower Brunswick aquifers, grouped as the Brunswick aquifer system (unit 3);

- the Upper Floridan confining unit (unit 4);

- the Upper Floridan aquifer (units 5);

- the Lower Floridan confining unit (unit 6); and

- the Lower Floridan aquifer (unit 7).

The refined model incorporates additional model layers to provide for local variations in hydraulic properties at Brunswick (fig. 43). This includes subdividing the Brunswick aquifer system (unit 3) into separate units for the upper and lower Brunswick aquifers and subdividing the Upper Floridan aquifer (unit 4) into upper and lower water-bearing zones as defined by Wait and Gregg (1974). Each new layer is separated from adjacent aquifers by a semiconfining unit. These changes were made in order to more accurately simulate the horizontal and vertical hydraulic gradients that have been documented for these units in the Brunswick–Glynn County area.

The original model (Payne and others, 2005) simulated steady-state conditions during predevelopment (pre-1900), 1980, and 2000. The refined model is being updated to include simulated conditions during 2004. Preliminary model results indicate that residuals between simulated and observed heads provide a reasonable match. Thus, the model can be used to evaluate a variety of groundwater management scenarios, and the resulting effect on the chloride plume and hydraulic gradients near the chloride plume (Cherry, 2009). The updated model is being used to evaluate potential effects of seven groundwater-management scenarios on hydraulic gradients near the chloride plume.

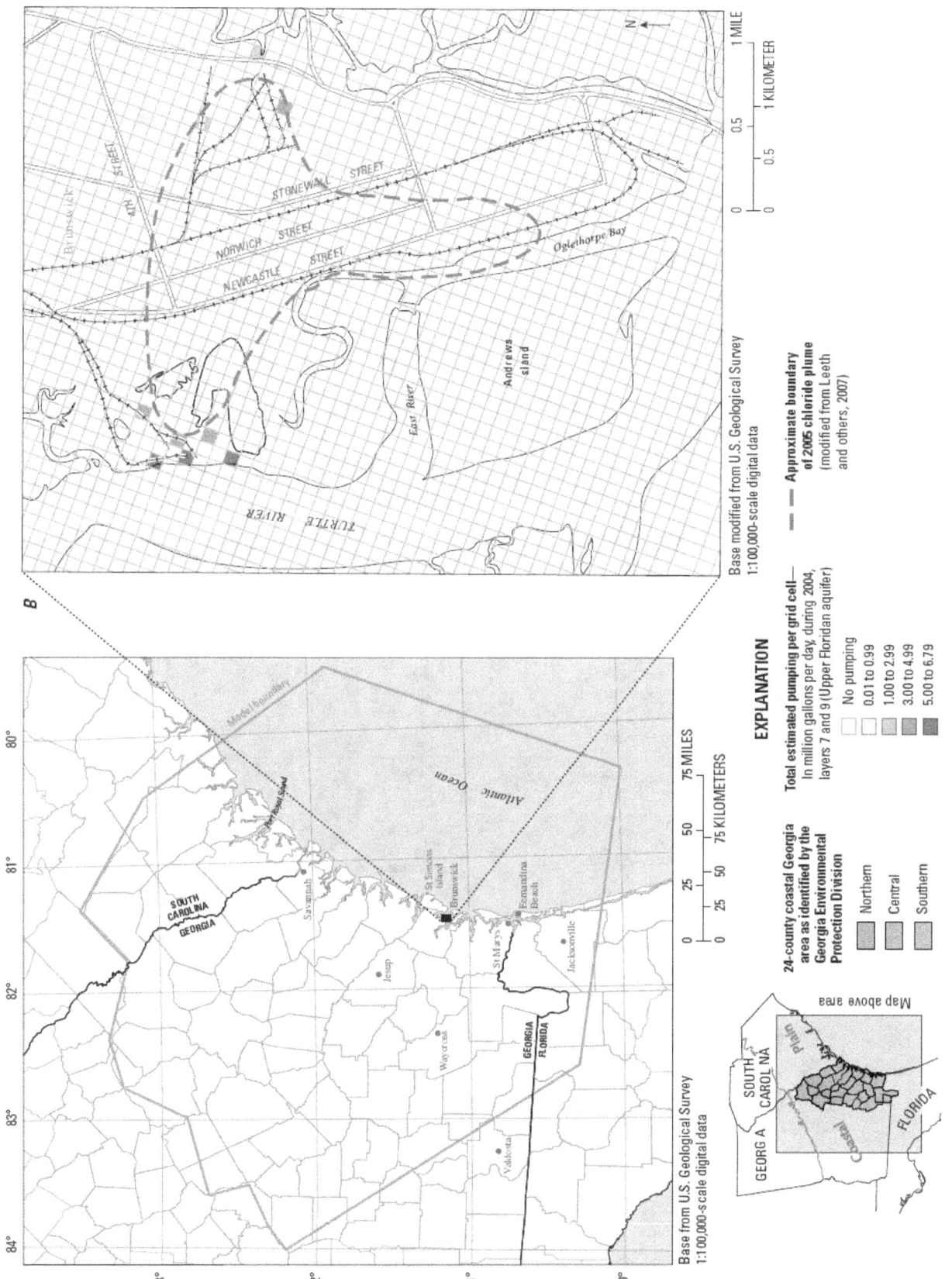

Figure 42. (A) Location of 24-county coastal Georgia area and model extent, and (B) model grid and distribution of pumpage by model layer for layers 7 and 9, Upper Floridan aquifer, Brunswick–Glynn County area, Georgia, 2004.

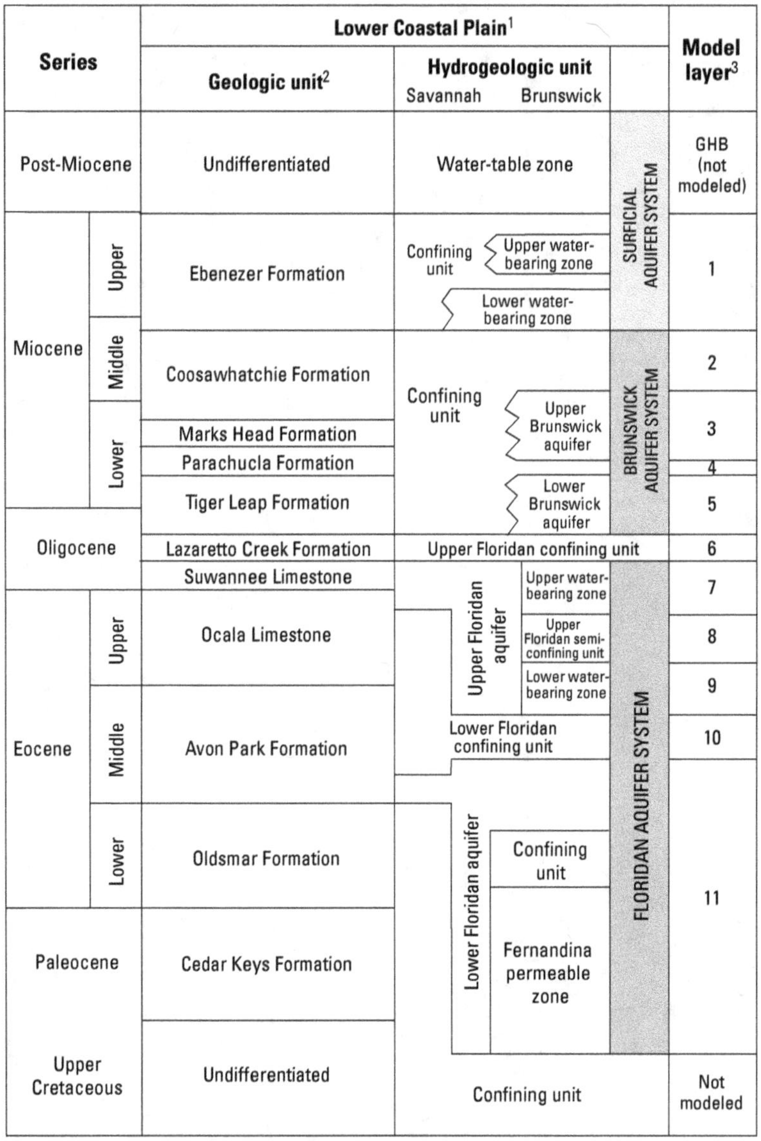

Series		Lower Coastal Plain[1]			Model layer[3]
		Geologic unit[2]	Hydrogeologic unit		
			Savannah	Brunswick	
Post-Miocene		Undifferentiated	Water-table zone	SURFICIAL AQUIFER SYSTEM	GHB (not modeled)
Miocene	Upper	Ebenezer Formation	Confining unit	Upper water-bearing zone	1
				Lower water-bearing zone	
	Middle	Coosawhatchie Formation	Confining unit		2
				Upper Brunswick aquifer	3
	Lower	Marks Head Formation			
		Parachucla Formation			4
		Tiger Leap Formation		Lower Brunswick aquifer	5
Oligocene		Lazaretto Creek Formation	Upper Floridan confining unit		6
		Suwannee Limestone	Upper Floridan aquifer	Upper water-bearing zone	7
Eocene	Upper	Ocala Limestone		Upper Floridan semi-confining unit	8
				Lower water-bearing zone	9
	Middle	Avon Park Formation	Lower Floridan confining unit		10
	Lower	Oldsmar Formation	Lower Floridan aquifer	Confining unit	11
Paleocene		Cedar Keys Formation		Fernandina permeable zone	
Upper Cretaceous		Undifferentiated	Confining unit		Not modeled

(BRUNSWICK AQUIFER SYSTEM; FLORIDAN AQUIFER SYSTEM)

[1] Modified from Randolph and others, 1991; Clarke and Krause, 2000
[2] Modified from Randolph and others, 1991; Weems and Edwards, 2001
[3] From Payne and others, 2005

Figure 43.   Generalized correlation of geologic and hydrogeologic units and model layers. [GHB, general-head boundary]

Reports and Technical Presentations

The USGS prepared several reports and technical presentations about coastal Georgia during 2008 and has provided technical briefings and progress reports at monthly meetings of the Glynn County Water Resources Management Advisory Committee (WRMAC). Recent reports and presentations on coastal Georgia include:

- USGS Open-File Report 1297, "Groundwater conditions and studies in the Brunswick–Glynn County area, Georgia, 2007," by Gregory S. Cherry and John S. Clarke (*http://pubs.usgs.gov/of/2008/1297/*)

- USGS Scientific Investigations Report 2009–5070, "Ground-water conditions and studies in Georgia, 2006–2007" by Michael F. Peck, Jaime A. Painter, and David C. Leeth (*http://pubs.usgs.gov/sir/2009/5070/*)

- Presentation at the 2008 Georgia Association of Water Professionals Spring Conference held in Columbus, GA, titled, "Optimization of groundwater pumping distribution to limit chloride plume expansion in the Upper Floridan aquifer near Brunswick, Georgia," by Gregory S. Cherry and Dorothy F. Payne

- Presentation at the 2008 Greater Atlanta Geomorphology and Hydrology Research Conference held in Atlanta, GA, titled, "Optimization of groundwater pumping distribution to limit chloride plume expansion in the Upper Floridan aquifer near Brunswick, Georgia," by Gregory S. Cherry and Dorothy F. Payne

Selected References

Barber, N.L., and Stamey, T.C., 2000, Droughts in Georgia: U.S. Geological Survey Open-File Report 00–380, 2 p., accessed September 5, 2008, at *http://pubs.usgs.gov/of/2000/0380/*.

Cherry, G.S., 2007, U.S. Geological Survey Georgia Water Science Center and City of Brunswick–Glynn County Cooperative Water Program—Summary of activities, July 2005 through June 2006: U.S. Geological Survey Open-File Report 2006–1368, 64 p., accessed May 19, 2008, at *http://pubs.usgs.gov/of/2006/1368/*.

Cherry, G.S., 2009, Groundwater modeling and monitoring to manage chloride plume expansion in the Upper Floridan aquifer near Brunswick, Georgia, *in* Carroll, G.D., ed., Proceedings of the 2009 Georgia Water Resources Conference, held April 27–29, 2009, at the University of Georgia, Athens, Institute of Ecology, The University of Georgia, accessed July 2, 2009, at *http://www.gwri.gatech.edu/uploads/proceedings/2009/6.3.3_Cherry.pdf.*

Cherry, G.S., and Clarke, J.S., 2008, Ground-water conditions and studies in the Brunswick–Glynn County area, Georgia, 2007: U.S. Geological Survey Open-File Report 2008–1297, 42 p., available online only at *http://pubs.usgs.gov/of/2008/1297/*.

Cherry, G.S., and Payne, D.F., 2007, Optimization of groundwater pumpage distribution to limit chloride plume expansion in the Upper Floridan aquifer near Brunswick, Georgia, *in* Rasmussen, Todd, Carroll, G.D., and Georgakakos, Aris, eds., Proceedings of the 2007 Georgia Water Resources Conference, held March 27–29, 2007, at the University of Georgia, Athens, Institute of Ecology, The University of Georgia, accessed May 20, 2008, at *http://ga.water.usgs.gov/publications/gwrc07/*.

Clarke, J.S., 2007, The monitoring and modeling approach to support groundwater management in Georgia, *in* Rasmussen, Todd, Carroll, G.D., and Georgakakos, Aris, eds., Proceedings of the 2007 Georgia Water Resources Conference, held March 27–29, 2007, at the University of Georgia, Athens, Institute of Ecology, The University of Georgia, accessed May 20, 2008, at *http://ga.water.usgs.gov/publications/gwrc07/*.

Clarke, J.S., Hacke, C.M., and Peck, M.F., 1990, Geology and groundwater resources of the coastal area of Georgia: Georgia Geologic Survey Bulletin 113, 106 p.

Clarke, J.S., and Krause, R.E., 2000, Design, revision, and application of groundwater flow models for simulation of selected water-management scenarios in the coastal area of Georgia and adjacent parts of South Carolina and Florida: U.S. Geological Survey Water-Resources Investigations Report 00–4084, 93 p.

Fanning, J.L., and Trent, V.P., 2009, Water use in Georgia by county for 2005; and water-use trends, 1980–2005: U.S. Geological Survey Scientific Investigations Report 2009–5002, 186 p., accessed May 29, 2009, at *http://pubs.usgs.gov/sir/2009/5002/*.

Georgia Environmental Protection Division, 1997, Secondary maximum contaminant levels for drinking water, Environmental Rule 391-3-5-19, revised October 1997: Official Code of Georgia Annotated Statutes, Statute 12–5–170 (Georgia Safe Drinking Water Act), variously paged.

Hall, M.E., and Peck, M.F., 2005, Saltwater contamination due to well construction problems—A case study from Vernonberg, Georgia, *in* Hatcher, K.J. ed., Proceedings of the 2005 Georgia Water Resources Conference, held April 25–27, 2005, at The University of Georgia, Athens, Institute of Ecology, The University of Georgia, accessed November 10, 2005, at *http://ga.water.usgs.gov/pubs/other/gwrc2005/*.

Hall, M.E., and Peck, M.F., 2007, Saltwater contamination in the Upper Floridan aquifer in the Savannah/Vernonburg, Georgia, area, 2004–2006, *in* Rasmussen, Todd, Carroll, G.D., and Georgakakos, Aris, eds., Proceedings of the 2007 Georgia Water Resources Conference, held March 27–29, 2007, at the University of Georgia, Athens, Institute of Ecology, The University of Georgia, accessed May 20, 2008, at *http://ga.water.usgs.gov/publications/gwrc07/*.

Harbaugh, A.W., Banta, E.R., Hill, M.C., and McDonald, M.G., 2000, MODFLOW-2000, the U.S. Geological Survey modular groundwater model—User guide to modularization concepts and the groundwater flow process: U.S. Geological Survey Open-File Report 00–92, 121 p.

Leeth, D.C., Peck, M.F., and Painter, J.A., 2007, Groundwater conditions and studies in Georgia, 2004–2005: U.S. Geological Survey Scientific Investigations Report 2007–5017, 299 p., accessed May 19, 2008, at *http://pubs.usgs.gov/sir/2007/5017/*.

Payne, D.F., 2007, Effects of pumpage reduction in the Savannah, Georgia–Hilton Head Island, South Carolina, area on saltwater intrusion near Hilton Head Island, *in* Rasmussen, Todd, Carroll, D.G., and Georgakakos, Aris, eds., Proceedings of the 2007 Georgia Water Resources Conference, held March 27–29, 2007, at the University of Georgia, Athens, Institute of Ecology, The University of Georgia, accessed May 20, 2008, at *http://ga.water.usgs.gov/publications/gwrc07/*.

Payne, D.F., Rumman M.A., and Clarke J.S., 2005, Simulation of groundwater flow in coastal Georgia and adjacent parts of South Carolina and Florida—Predevelopment, 1980, and 2000: U.S. Geological Survey Scientific Investigations Report 2005–5089, 91 p., accessed January 18, 2006, at *http://pubs.usgs.gov/sir/2005/5089/*.

Peck, M.F., Painter, J.A., and Leeth, D.C., 2009 Groundwater conditions and studies in Georgia, 2006–2007: U.S. Geological Survey Scientific Investigations Report 2009–5070, 86 p.

Randolph, R.B., Pernik, M., and Garza, R., 1991, Water supply potential of the Floridan aquifer system in the coastal area of Georgia—A digital model approach: Georgia Geologic Survey Bulletin 116, 30 p.

U.S. Environmental Protection Agency, 2000 revised, Maximum contaminant levels (Part 143, National Secondary Drinking-Water Regulations): U.S. Code of Federal Regulations, Title 40, parts 100–149.

Wait, R.L., 1965, Geology and occurrence of fresh and brackish groundwater in Glynn County, Georgia: U.S. Geological Survey Water-Supply Paper 1613-E, 94 p.

Wait, R.L., and Gregg, D.O., 1974, Hydrology and chloride contamination of the principal artesian aquifer in Glynn County, Georgia Department of Natural Resources Hydrologic Report, 93 p.

Walls, C.B., Cressler, A.M., and Stayton, W.L., 2009, Real-time water-level and specific conductance monitoring of saltwater contamination in the Upper Floridan aquifer, Brunswick, Georgia, *in* Carroll, D.G., ed., Proceedings of the 2009 Georgia Water Resources Conference, held April 27–29, 2009, at the University of Georgia, Athens, Institute of Ecology, The University of Georgia, accessed July 2, 2009.

Weems, R.E., and Edwards, L.E., 2001, Geology, of Oligocene, Miocene, and younger deposits in the coastal area of Georgia: Georgia Geologic Survey Bulletin 131, 124 p.

Manuscript approved on November 30, 2009

For more information about this publication contact:

Director
USGS Georgia Water Science Center
3039 Amwiler Road, Suite 130
Atlanta, GA 30360
Telephone: 770-903-9100
http://ga.water.usgs.gov